## Praise for *Ask Outrageously!*

"It's only outrageous if you don't ask! The bigger the ask, the bigger the reward. It all starts by digging in and reading *Ask Outrageously!*"
—**Mark Hunter, CSP, "The Sales Hunter," author of *High-Profit Prospecting***

"Linda Swindling's new book is a winner! If you read only one book this year, get it, read it, learn the content, and reap new rewards."
—**Don Hutson, CEO, US Learning, and coauthor of the *New York Times* #1 bestseller *The One Minute Entrepreneur***

"Linda has nailed the way to get better results: ask outrageously up front. Trust me—read the book!"
—**David Horsager, bestselling author and CEO, Trust Edge Leadership Institute**

"Love this book and the premise of 'just ask' and you shall receive. Asking for what you want translates across cultures."
—**Daisy Chin-Lor, President, Tupperware and Nutrimetics Australia and New Zealand**

"Linda understands how to ask—that's why she has my endorsement!"
—**Ed Brodow, author of *Negotiation Boot Camp***

"Wow! Linda's book whacked me between the eyes. I recommend it to all CEOs and C-suite leaders."
—**Stephen Tweed, CEO, Leading Home Care**

"Linda's book covers substantive content that can enable you to do more, be more, and achieve more. Read it to learn. Apply it to succeed."
—**Dr. Nido R. Qubein, President, High Point University**

"To reach your desired pinnacle, it is crucial to ask outrageously."
—**Frances Rios, founder of Latin America's Women Who Lead Summit**

"When you're ready to stop playing it safe, start asking outrageously."
—**Elizabeth McCormick, former US Army Black Hawk Pilot and author of *The PILOT Method* and the Soar 2 Success Business Series**

"Follow Linda's advice. In one year, her strategies helped one of my companies add $3 million to the bottom line."
—**David Irons, Senior Vice President, Sales and Marketing, Perfection Learning Corporation**

"Want to make your message memorable? Good. *Ask Outrageously!*"
—**Patricia Fripp, President, A Speaker for All Reasons**

"Linda provides the flight plan to ask when it matters most."
—**Howard Putnam, former CEO, Southwest Airlines, and author of *The Winds of Turbulence***

"Linda is a communication ninja and a master requester. Read this book."
—**Kevin Jost, President, J&S Audio Visual**

"Want to level the playing field? Then ask and get your message heard."
—**Kate Delany, NBC syndicated talk show host and sports commentator**

"Everything *is* negotiable. But you have to ask. Linda shows you how."
—**John Patrick Dolan, JD, author of *Negotiate Like the Pros***

"Asking feels so much better than constantly wondering *what if*."
—**Kip Eads, CAE, Vice President, Professional Development, Professional Retail Store Maintenance Association**

"To be financially successful, you have to ask the hard questions. This book helps you peel back the onion to the core issues holding you back."
—**Mitch Kramer, CFP, founder and CEO, Fluent Financial, Inc.**

"People will freely give their wisdom and support, but most of us won't ask. Read this book to squarely place you on your path to success."
—**Joseph Sherren, author and Professor, York University Business School**

"Outrageously good! To stand out, ask outrageously."
—**Connie Podesta, coauthor of *Ten Ways to Stand Out from the Crowd***

"Linda shows you powerful ways to ask for more...and get it!"
—**Roger Dawson, author of *Secrets of Power Negotiating***

"This book is a primer for your personal and professional life. Read it if you want to increase your earnings and make your customers proud."
—**Jim Eckelberger, Rear Admiral, US Navy (Ret.), Chairman of the Board, Southwest Power Pool**

"Ask boldly. Be outrageous; it's the only place that isn't crowded!"™
—**Mikki Williams, Producer, Speakers School, and Master Chair, Vistage**

"Ask outrageously? Yep. Linda is the expert. *Believe me.*"
—**Gregg Swindling, Linda's husband of more than twenty-five years**

# Ask
*Outrageously!*

# Ask
# *Outrageously!*

## The Secret to Getting What You Really Want

### LINDA BYARS SWINDLING

**BK**

Berrett–Koehler Publishers, Inc.
*a BK Life book*

**Berrett-Koehler Publishers, Inc.**
1333 Broadway, Suite 1000
Oakland, CA 94612-1921
Tel: (510) 817-2277     Fax: (510) 817-2278     www.bkconnection.com

**Ordering Information**
**Quantity sales.** Special discounts are available on quantity purchases by corporations, associations, and others. For details, contact the "Special Sales Department" at the Berrett-Koehler address above.
**Individual sales.** Berrett-Koehler publications are available through most bookstores. They can also be ordered directly from Berrett-Koehler: Tel: (800) 929-2929; Fax: (802) 864-7626; www.bkconnection.com
**Orders for college textbook/course adoption use.** Please contact Berrett-Koehler: Tel: (800) 929-2929; Fax: (802) 864-7626.
**Orders by U.S. trade bookstores and wholesalers.** Please contact Ingram Publisher Services:` Tel: (800) 509-4887; Fax: (800) 838-1149; E-mail: customer.service@ingrampublisherservices.com; or visit www.ingrampublisherservices.com/Ordering for details about electronic ordering.

Berrett-Koehler and the BK logo are registered trademarks of Berrett-Koehler Publishers, Inc.

Printed in the United States of America

Berrett-Koehler books are printed on long-lasting acid-free paper. When it is available, we choose paper that has been manufactured by environmentally responsible processes. These may include using trees grown in sustainable forests, incorporating recycled paper, minimizing chlorine in bleaching, or recycling the energy produced at the paper mill.

ISBN 978-1-5230-8271-1

Library of Congress Cataloging-in-Publication Data
A catalog record for this book is available from the Library of Congress

First Edition
21  20  19  18  17          10  9  8  7  6  5  4  3  2  1

Project management, design, and composition by Steven Hiatt, Hiatt & Dragon, San Francisco
Copyeditor: Susan Lang   Proofreader: Tom Hassett   Indexer: Theresa Duran   Cover designer: Susan Malikowski, DesignLeaf Studio

To my outrageous family and friends, thank you for all you do and who you are. To my clients, to the wonderful professionals who attend my programs, and to those who read the words in this book, be courageous and seek those outrageous outcomes.

You deserve to get what you really want.

# Contents

# Introduction

# Ask Outrageously!

*Can you keep a secret?*
If you don't have what you really want in your life right now, you probably haven't asked or you are settling for less than what is available.

*Want to know more?*
The number of opportunities you miss concerns me. From my experience and research, I know you overlook possibilities well within your reach. When you make requests, you overprepare and focus on areas that don't get results or a yes. Despite your preparation, experience, and ability, you ignore what matters most.

*Want proof?*
Examine the recent research. More than a thousand people (1,163 to be accurate) from a wide variety of professions participated in our Ask Outrageously Study. They revealed what prevents them from asking for what they want and the areas in which they weren't effective when asking. Their responses uncovered major flaws in what we request and how we ask. The

data spotlighted big misunderstandings about why people say no. One reason I wanted to write this book was to break these misperceptions and shed light on why your efforts don't work. I also wanted to let you know that you are not alone. According to our study, 80 percent of us say that we could enhance our results by improving how we ask. The remaining 20 percent say that they ask effectively. Many of their responses imply they wonder why the others do not ask when given the opportunity.

### What's the bottom line?

You stop yourself from making better requests and getting better results. From my experience, backed by our research, I can tell you that you are getting in your own way. Instead, you need to feel the fear—and then ask anyway.

### Be the first to ask.

Imagine sitting in the studio audience of *The Tonight Show* with then-host Jay Leno. Jay comes out before the taping and asks for questions from the audience. Surprisingly, he picks you to ask him a question first. This happened to me. I had two questions: first, I asked about his job, and then I was going to ask for a picture with him on the stage.

Jay responded to my first question. Before I could ask for my picture, he turned and answered another woman's question. She asked for what I really wanted, a picture with him. As she made her way to the stage, Jay turned back at me. He said, "That's what you wanted to ask for, isn't it? A picture." I nodded and started rising from my chair. He gestured for me to stay seated. Shaking his head, he said words I'll never forget: "Sorry. You didn't *ask*. She did."

Thinking about that day still gives me a sinking feeling. Instead of asking for what I really wanted first, I delayed and put unnecessary effort into finding out information I didn't need. I'm not alone in failing to ask for what I really wanted. Our study showed that one-third of people wanted to ask for something big but didn't. They waited to ask for a raise, a promotion, moving expenses, and even spending money in college. Later, they saw someone else get what they wanted. Like me, they thought about making that request, but didn't follow through or waited to get more information.

*Do your own asking.*

When our daughter, Taylor, was four, we took her to a school carnival. There she spotted the face-painting booth and told us, "I want my face painted. I want a butterfly." My husband, Gregg, said, "Great. Here's a ticket. Go ask them for what you want. Your mom and I will wait." Taylor had a different idea. She wanted us to ask the booth volunteers for her. After much protesting and pleading on her part, my husband bent down. He looked her straight in the eye and told her, "Mommy and I don't want our faces painted. We don't want a butterfly. You do. If you want *your* face painted, *you* have to ask. We'll be here watching. You will be OK."

Reluctantly, Taylor walked over to the booth. When her face was painted, she skipped back to us. Taylor was happy about her purple and pink butterfly and proud of herself for asking. She spent the rest of the night asking for what she wanted at other booths. Although it would have been easy for us to ask on her behalf, our preschooler learned a valuable lesson that many adults struggle with: *you have to do your own asking.*

Asking is not a task to be delegated or avoided. You can't wait for someone to recognize that you deserve better or to speak for you. When I practiced law, I strongly negotiated and made requests for others. Rarely, though, did I ask for what I needed or really wanted. Although I acted in the best interests of my clients, my attempts to avoid looking greedy or self-absorbed were not in *my* best interest. Honestly, people would have been delighted to help me if I had asked. My clients received great results. However, my failure to ask blocked me from possibilities that were appropriate and attainable for me.

### *Ask outside your comfort zone.*

My first months in law school were miserable. Those days, I questioned my intelligence and decision to attend. Worse, I sat in classrooms with other students who appeared to understand the lectures. Many of my peers would nod intelligently. A few offered comments to show their grasp of the material.

My classroom strategy was different from that of those confident legal scholars. My plan was to hide my ignorance, avoid drawing attention to myself, and hope the professors didn't call on me to answer questions.

There was additional pressure to stay silent. Some of my peers reacted negatively to a student brave enough to ask "stupid" questions. This elite group would smirk. They rolled their eyes and shook their heads at the student's ignorance. The condescending looks created a chilling effect. Each day, I was afraid of professional embarrassment *before* I was a legal professional. So I hid, took copious notes, and prayed for enlightenment that never came.

One day in my contracts class I felt particularly frustrated and confused. After an internal debate, I decided it would be more expensive and embarrassing to fail law school than to ask a question. Timidly, I raised my hand and asked our professor about the concept of "promissory estoppel."

Guess what? He was happy to answer. He said it was "a fairly common question." With his explanation, the concept wasn't confusing at all. After a month of sitting silently, avoiding eye contact, and feeling intimidated, asking a question finally helped me grasp a legal concept. Understanding was a tremendous relief. The results of stretching outside my comfort zone outweighed the embarrassment. A few professors became mentors once they saw I was interested in understanding the law. Surprisingly, I formed friendships with other confused classmates and several upper-level students. As an added benefit, I found that upper-classmen can tell you about professors and share notes from their first year.

Yes, comments and jokes were made regarding my "stupid" questions and lack of intelligence. Know what? None of those snickering students had the power to give me a grade, grant me an internship, or pay my bills. Once unleashed, I began asking all the time. Outrageously, I asked two famous authors to attend receptions at our law school and *speak for free* when they came to our university. Guess what? Both feminist Gloria Steinem and Sarah Weddington, a former member of the Texas House of Representatives, agreed to my request. Asking questions and being vulnerable helped me make better grades, rank higher in my class, and land a job when I completed law school.

How does a preschooler's reluctance to approach a carnival booth or a law student's fear of asking questions relate to you? Turns out the answer is plenty. Asking outrageously feels intimidating and uncomfortable to the person making the request. Many of us stop ourselves before asking because the request doesn't feel safe. We are concerned about what others think of us or how prepared we are.

*You don't know what you don't know.*
Elaine Morris, the business coach I hired to help me grow my law practice, asked me a question years ago. "We've doubled your

revenue. You spend more time with your family, yet you still don't seem happy. If you could do more of anything, without worrying about money, what would it be?" I answered that I loved presenting at conferences and the training I did for free. She replied, "You know, people get paid good money for that, right?" No, I didn't. I thought only teachers and professors were paid to teach. I figured the rest of the experts spoke for free to get more clients. Elaine sent me to the National Speakers Association. There, I met several professionals who had transitioned from other areas of business including law and now made a living by presenting, writing, and speaking.

---

## How can you know someone's answer to a question you haven't asked?

---

*Don't assume you know their answer.*
Years ago, I called a publisher to complain about a leadership program. I was transferred several times and finally was forwarded to "a leader who would be able to help fix my issue." After resolving the issue, he asked why a lawyer was interested in a leadership and communication program. During our conversation, we discussed my transition from practicing law to creating executive development programs. Before we hung up, I "outrageously" asked if he ever needed new authors.

Let's be clear. The request wasn't inappropriate or rude. However, it was outrageous *for me* because it was outside my concept of the norm. Asking the editor of a publishing house is not the traditional way books are submitted for consideration. I *know* you're *not supposed* to call up an editor and propose a book. There is a format to submit a proposal. And yet I asked even though I knew better.

Your comfort zone does not define how someone will respond to your request. My request was simply another question to the editor. Yet this outrageous ask gave me an outrageous outcome. This one request led to a published book and then several others. That conversation and the relationships that resulted from that one request became key to launching an executive development company and my professional speaking career twenty years ago. Imagine the power you could have if you felt the fear and asked anyway, without worrying or questioning yourself.

*Be courageous.*
The fearless have no problem asking. Our son, Parker, has always been a master at making requests. Once, while waiting at a restaurant, we turned around to find him missing. A few frantic minutes later, we saw him sitting in the restaurant eating pizza with a family who had a boy his age. When we went to reclaim our son, we asked how the two boys knew each other. School? Church? Scouts? "Nope." The mom laughed. "We just met Parker. He asked if he could join us and told us he was hungry."

As an adult and accountant-to-be, Parker continues his fearless requests. He asked his wife, Victoria, to marry him at a concert. More precisely, he asked her in the middle of the concert … by singing a solo to her … from the stage … in front of a packed auditorium, including several of his friends and a live-streamed audience. There's more to his outrageous request. A few days prior to the event, he asked the conductor and the band if he could interrupt *their* concert and propose by singing *his* favorite song. Oh, and could they learn the music to accompany him? Thankfully, the outcome was good. The band agreed. And she said yes.

Do you know people who ask all the time, without hesitation? Watch them. They may be young children who wear you down with their questions until you say yes. Maybe they are friends, a significant other, or a salesperson. Perhaps they run their own businesses, are decision makers in associations, work as service providers, or request funds on behalf of non-profit organizations. *They regularly ask outside most people's comfort zone, and they often get what they want.*

### Remember to ask.

Conducting the research for this book required an outrageous ask from me. It was ten days before the meeting with the publisher and two weeks before my TEDxSMU talk on this topic. During both presentations, I was presenting the final findings of our Ask Outrageously Study. The problem was that we hadn't reached our goal of 800 research responses. After three months, 562 participants had given us great suggestions, but that total fell short of the sampling size I wanted. Unlike the past two studies for books I had written, this survey was not gaining ground and time was running out.

Finally, I posted my issue in a social media group. Putting all pride aside, I asked my female speaking colleagues what actions they would take to hit the 800 goal. And I confessed I had only a short time frame. Can you guess what question they asked me?

Yep. They wanted to know, "Have you just asked?" Honestly, my answer was no. Consider the irony for a moment. I was speaking and writing about how to ask outrageously, yet I hadn't asked others for help. My friends told me what I tell others: ask people directly for their help. Don't try to provide information and value first. Lose the fluff. Don't hide the request. *Instead, just ask for what you really want.*

In a matter of minutes, one of my speaking friends had drafted a sample request for me. She told me to tag friends and ask them to tag ten of their friends. Even though I didn't want to bother people and I felt uncomfortable asking, I took a breath and posted my request. And then I witnessed the power of asking outrageously in action. Within days we hit the 800 mark and then unbelievably 1,000. A week later, we closed down the study with 1,163. My being a little vulnerable and asking more than doubled the results.

For years, I've watched myself, my clients, and people I love fail to ask or settle for less than we wanted. So, I started probing and did the research.

*I wrote this book on how to ask outrageously because:*

- I was curious and furious that the people I care about often go overlooked and unrewarded for their efforts and talents. I wanted to correct misconceptions about why their requests don't get a positive response and to help them focus on what really matters.

- I wanted to acknowledge those who taught me the power of being courageous, outrageous, and stretching outside my comfort zone. I also needed reminding of the power that comes from being vulnerable and asking for help.

- I wished that this book had existed years ago for me to read. Knowing how to request without reservation would have saved me thousands of dollars. The energy I spent could have been used in much more productive ways. Asking outrageously would have helped me avoid years of uncertainty, self-doubt, and the headaches resulting from trial and error.

- I learned through the years that leaders, mentors, and coaches want to help people they lead. They care about people's growth and development and about achieving success. (*Outrageous Request Alert*: How much more effective could your people be if they understood how to ask? What would be possible if you gave a copy of this book to all those you manage and influence?)

I hope the strategies and insights will shortcut your learning. It's important to know you can dramatically improve your ability to make requests. Also, I know you can influence not only your situation but create opportunities for others in a way only you can.

*Ask Outrageously!*
Linda

# How to Get Outrageous Results from This Book

### Define "Outrageous"
According to Merriam-Webster, "outrageous" means "Exceeding the limits of what is usual ... Not conventional or matter-of-fact: fantastic."

For the purposes of this book, "ask outrageously" is defined as making a request outside *your* comfort zone. There is a difference between outrageous and obnoxious. Nowhere will you see a suggestion to be negative or deceitful, or to take advantage of others. Instead, people who ask outrageously are surprised by the *positive* outcomes and *relationships* that result from requesting more than usual.

### *Where did this idea begin?*
Years ago, a client asked me to work with a group of high-level sales professionals. He was frustrated with several poor performers who argued, made excuses, and refused to ask clients to consider the company's new product. Fed up, my client and I decided to create an "asking" contest. We added an extra hour to their lunch, split them into small groups, gave each group $20, and sent them to an upscale mall next to the resort. Their challenge was simple: "Go ask for more and report your results to the group."

When the teams displayed their results, the difference was shocking. One group opted out and went to a bar. Another group added $10 of its own money and took advantage of a cosmetics promotion. One group purchased a buy-one-get-one-free offer for a dinner and increased their amount to $40. The last two groups returned with items totaling well over $100. By asking for samples, discounts, and freebies, they creatively out-requested their peers. (Guess which two groups had the better sales professionals and were highly successful with the new product that year.)

The challenge has been refined. Although many of the reported results are small, some are remarkable. Under a short deadline with few guidelines other than "go ask and report your results," attendees at all levels in a variety of professions achieved outrageous outcomes. For example, they:

- Asked for and were granted raises and promotions.
- Asked and repaired or elevated personal relationships.
- Asked and created a new business or established new lines of business.
- Asked for and received goods and services they could not otherwise afford.
- Asked for and recovered debt or reduced business expenses.
- Asked for and were given real estate property, including a house and a building.

With additional training, tools, and coaching, people continued to ask and received outcomes that surpassed anyone's expectations. Most of them credited their successes to new insights about communicating powerfully and being challenged to ask outrageously.

### If You Have No Difficulties Asking, Do You Need This Book?

You may be among the 20 percent who say that they are already very good at asking and get what they want most of the time.

Perhaps you are thinking something like the following:

- "I already know how to ask for what I want and I usually get it."
- "Really? People don't ask for things? What's their problem?"
- "What's the bottom line? I have work to get done."

You know how to identify and approach those with authority. And when it comes to asking, you have no fear. At times, you push the envelope with your requests. You may even treat asking as a challenge or game. You get great results and have a proven track record. If you have no difficulties asking, here are a few reasons to continue reading:

- You lead others. You can't determine why your people won't simply ask for a sale, close a deal, ask for a discount, or fix an ongoing problem.
- Someone you care about won't address a conflict, talk to a leader, ask for a raise, solve an issue, or get what they deserve.
- You received feedback that people don't always relate to, connect with, or trust you. Perhaps you've heard you are too tough on others, or you've received feedback about improving collaboration, growing your people, or forming better internal or external relationships.
- Agreements you thought were made and understood aren't. You can't let down your guard. You need to monitor details and watch people to make sure they uphold their commitments and promises.
- You know others could be more forthcoming, creative, or helpful. Yet you feel as if you are making all the effort with people who aren't supportive and don't care as much as you do.

Lead Others to Ask sections are found at the end of every chapter immediately before the Outrageous Reviews. Leaders may want to see the Outrageous Reviews at the end of each chapter as an executive summary complete with tools to help you implement.

After reading this book, you will be better prepared to determine when and what to ask. You will be exposed to the best ways to request what you want at work and in life with confidence and integrity. This book provides steps to reach breakthrough results and ask for more than you believe possible.

### What's in the book?

This book provides proven principles and ideas to help you show up powerfully and ask outrageously. These strategies and recommendations are supported by my more than twenty-five years' experience making high-stakes requests and helping people. Included are secrets and insights to help you understand the "why" behind some people's actions.

Each chapter offers engaging questions and actionable tips to help you get started. Instead of theories or philosophical ideas, you'll learn specific techniques and find tools to help you remember what to do under pressure. There are checklists to assist you in preparing and suggested conversations with scripted language to help you ask with confidence and in a way that makes people listen.

**Scenarios.** In the pages that follow, you'll find reports of the asking challenge, client stories, and other short, real-world examples of people who asked for and received more than they thought they deserved. In some cases, the names or details have been changed to protect the innocent (and the guilty), but the facts and outcomes are real and repeatable.

**Ask Outrageously Study.** Throughout this book, you'll see references to a study on how people ask and what holds them back. That study, conducted electronically over a four-month period, was designed to collect information about how people make requests. Respondents were given the option to take the survey anonymously. Their answers were insightful and reflected the difficulty most people have in making requests. Participants reported no significant differences in making personal and professional requests. Many provided encouragement to others to ask more powerfully and to receive better results.

The 1,163 survey participants came from professions within twenty-one occupational categories in a wide variety of industries (see Figure 1). The most common professional fields participating in the research were sales, marketing, and public relations—fields in which practitioners earn a living making requests.

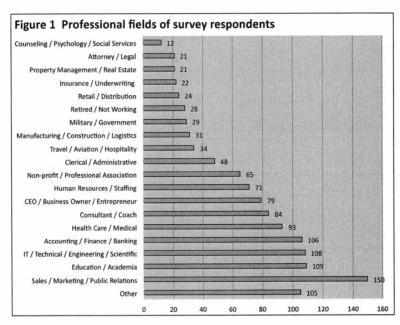

**Figure 1  Professional fields of survey respondents**

| Field | Count |
|---|---|
| Counseling / Psychology / Social Services | 12 |
| Attorney / Legal | 21 |
| Property Management / Real Estate | 21 |
| Insurance / Underwriting | 22 |
| Retail / Distribution | 24 |
| Retired / Not Working | 28 |
| Military / Government | 29 |
| Manufacturing / Construction / Logistics | 31 |
| Travel / Aviation / Hospitality | 34 |
| Clerical / Administrative | 48 |
| Non-profit / Professional Association | 65 |
| Human Resources / Staffing | 71 |
| CEO / Business Owner / Entrepreneur | 79 |
| Consultant / Coach | 84 |
| Health Care / Medical | 93 |
| Accounting / Finance / Banking | 106 |
| IT / Technical / Engineering / Scientific | 108 |
| Education / Academia | 109 |
| Sales / Marketing / Public Relations | 150 |
| Other | 105 |

The survey contained a mix of open-ended and multiple choice (single- and multiple-select) questions with an ability to provide optional comments. Survey responses are presented throughout the book in the form of graphs, respondent quotes, descriptions, suggestions, and experiences woven into scenarios. Unless otherwise designated, mentions of research, study findings, and survey participants refer to the Ask Outrageously Study. Full results are available at AskOutrageously.com.

**Quotes.** Unless otherwise indicated, *italicized text* indicates quotes provided by participants in the Ask Outrageously Study as well as feedback from our program participants, audience members, and clients.

**Outrageous Review.** At the end of each chapter, you'll find an executive summary with highlights of the chapter. You can read the entire book and look at the summaries later as reference. If you prefer, skim through the book using the reviews and explore just the sections that interest you now.

 **Smart Asks.** At the end of the chapters you'll find questions to help you ask with more confidence and have fewer regrets.

 **Ask List.** Task lists are so last decade. Instead, add these outrageous asks to your to-do list. All of these requests are safe and proven to upgrade your results. When you practice asking outside your comfort zone, you prove to yourself that you can be more successful by asking outrageously. Accept these challenges to become a master of requests.

 **Secret Success Tools.** In addition, you have access to supporting resources on the website AskOutrageously.com. Use these tips, materials, and tools to dramatically improve your requests.

**Lead Others to Ask.** A twist on the often-recommended "Ask to Lead," this section contains suggestions for developing the people you supervise, mentor, or coach to ask more powerfully. These techniques help you delegate request making. They are designed to address the question "I'm great at making requests. How do I coach *others* to ask and get the results I do?"

**Take the Assessment.** Before reading further, please take the free assessment How Well Do You Ask? on page 18. You can also take the assessment online at AskOutrageously.com. The online version will direct you to additional tools.

If you think you already ask outrageously, the results will either confirm or challenge your perception. Now, are you ready for an outrageous request, or if you prefer, a dare? See if you are as good at asking as you think you are. Take the assessment. The results may surprise you.

Using proven strategies, you can dramatically improve your ability to be heard, to be seriously considered, and to influence powerfully.

Are you ready to be a smart ask and maximize your results? Great! Read on to ask outrageously!

# Assessment: How Well Do You Ask?

For each statement, choose rating that best reflects your current negotiating skill level. If you would rate yourself differently between work and home, select the lower rating. Then add up all the ratings for your total score.

**Use this scale for rating:**
**1 = *Never* 2 = *Rarely* 3 = *Sometimes* 4 = *Usually* 5 = *Always***

| Currently when I ask, I ... | Rating |
|---|---|
| Boldly request what I really want without fear or hesitation. Nothing stops or blocks me from asking. | |
| Make requests benefiting me with the same passion and confidence I make requests on behalf of others. | |
| Know people like and respect me. They trust my motives and know I honor my word. They willingly support our agreement even if I'm not present. | |
| Ask the right person, in the right way, and easily tailor my approach no matter whom I encounter. I am not intimidated by another's title, role, or experience. | |
| Know my request is appropriate, even if the request is unpopular, untried, or a new concept. I am certain the person I ask has the ability to approve my requests. | |
| Remain calm and in control despite others' reactions, negative behavior, or responses including no. I am fully prepared to deal with any tricks or unfair tactics. | |
| Regularly receive results that exceed what I wanted or thought possible. I am completely satisfied with my outcomes and confident I leave nothing on the table. | |

**Total score:**_____

**35 = You get what you really want and what everyone else wants too!**

**28–34 = You usually get what you want.**

**21–27 = You sometimes get what you want and sometimes not.**

**13–20 = You want to get a whole lot more.**

**7–13 = You seldom get what you want and wonder why.**

# One

# Proof You Should Ask Outrageously

There is magic in asking. The people with the best results are those who have the courage to feel the fear and ask anyway. They win more by being willing to push the envelope. They learn to ask for a little more and explore possibilities. They become more comfortable with taking risks and even hearing no.

People in history—from politicians to rock stars to Nobel Peace Prize winners—have had great success making outrageous requests. Having the courage to ask creates unbelievable results. A simple request can challenge injustice in the name of human dignity, generate significant medical advancements, create new ways of doing business, and impact communities. Consider these historic requests.

> Rosa Parks *asked*, "Why do I have to sit at the back of the bus?" and her request led to changing racial segregation laws to protect the rights of all citizens regardless of race.

> Louis Pasteur *asked*, "What causes wine to sour?"—a request that led to the discovery of how to destroy bacteria, which evolved into pasteurization technology to keep food safe.

Mary-Ellis Bunim and Jonathan Murray *asked* MTV, "Can we create an unscripted television show that follows the life of strangers in a house?" The result led to *The Real World* and the genre of reality TV. (Arguably, some results are more notable than others.)

## Outrageous Outcomes

There is a snowball effect when you begin to ask outrageously. What may be a simple request often grows into several requests. Asking can evolve into negotiations involving bigger stakes than you thought possible.

Want a secret only those who make high-stakes requests know? Asking outrageously feels the same, no matter the dollar amount or the consequences. The adrenaline rush, the fear, the excitement, the quickening heartbeat, the change in breathing, and the concentrated attention *feel the same*. And people who ask outrageously receive unbelievable results in all areas of their lives. Often, the most meaningful outcomes are personal ones.

*After years of no communication, I called my son and apologized. I asked if we could start over. He let me speak to my grandson for the first time. My grandson is four years old.*

*I asked my boyfriend when he thought we should get married. He proposed the next week. He had paid for the ring six months ago but didn't think I was ready and was waiting.*

*I asked my parents if I could borrow the money to make a down payment on a house. Instead of loaning it to me, they* **gave** *me the money. They had wanted to help me but didn't know how. I'd still be living in an apartment if I hadn't asked.*

Other outrageous outcomes begin with requests that are business related:

*I asked my partners if they were willing to expand by opening an office in San Antonio or Austin. They agreed and we opened offices in both cities.*

*After seventeen years of thinking about it, I approached physicians in other medical practices. I asked if they were interested in how we handled our back office and our methods for collecting payments. That request led to an entirely new business, which has generated millions of dollars.*

*In the past, a supplier and I did a lot of business together, but we had a falling out. I went to her booth on the trade show floor and asked if we could put our grievances aside and do business again. We just filled our largest order yet.*

*During a break in the negotiations seminar, I went into the hall and made a call to ask for a reduction in our medical equipment rental fees. We now are paying 30 percent less for the same equipment. I locked down the price for the next three years, and it only took one phone call.*

### What's Difficult about Asking?

More than 96 percent of those surveyed said they could have improved their results by asking for a little bit more or by taking more of a risk (see Figure 2). Almost a third said they could have increased their results by at least 50 percent. According to the study, the top reasons people hold back or don't ask are:

- *I will frustrate or bug the person I'm asking.*
- *I will use the wrong words.*
- *I will embarrass myself or look stupid.*
- *I will be told no.*

This self-monitoring and reluctance to ask prevents you from receiving results well within your grasp. And "overwhelm or bug

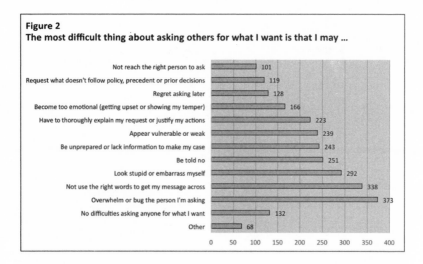

**Figure 2**
**The most difficult thing about asking others for what I want is that I may …**

the person I'm asking" ranks as significantly more difficult than "be told no." Seems odd, right? People would rather be told no than feel they are bothering someone to get what they want.

The Ask Outrageously Study reveals people are worried about the wrong things. For instance, people think their requests are denied because:

- *The other person lacks all the information needed.*
- *The timing is wrong.*
- *The person I'm asking doesn't want to spend the money.*

Actually, the top two reasons people report saying no when approached are that the person making the request:

- *Is asking for something that is inappropriate.*
- *Is someone I don't like, respect, or trust.*

News flash: We are focusing on the wrong things. The research shows that there is no correlation between why people *say* no and why people *think* they are told no. Most people don't know the true reasons that their requests have been denied.

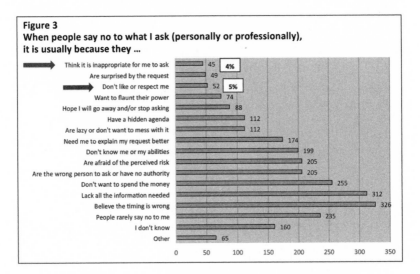

**Figure 3**
**When people say no to what I ask (personally or professionally), it is usually because they ...**

The primary reason people *say* no is when a person "is asking for something inappropriate" (with 36 percent reporting it as the primary reason). However, when given the opportunity to select "inappropriate" as a reason their requests are denied, only 4 percent of people *thought* it was the answer. (See Figure 4.)

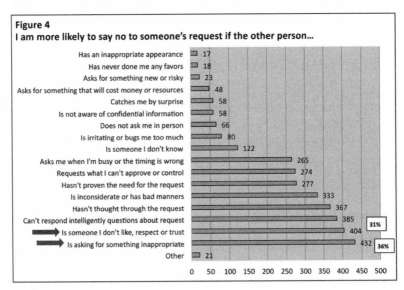

**Figure 4**
**I am more likely to say no to someone's request if the other person...**

To further support this disparity, 31 percent of respondents report saying no if they "don't like, trust, or respect" the person making the request. However, only 5 percent of people *think* that they're told no because the people they've asked "don't like or respect me."

The study also showed 79 percent of people feel more confident and prepared when they have all the information needed.

What a tremendous disconnect between perception and reality! What good is preparing with all the information needed when you are asking the wrong person for the wrong thing? How does all that research data help when the person you ask doesn't like, respect, or trust you?

### What are the consequences of not asking?

Not getting what you want or living with outcomes determined by someone else is draining. Patiently waiting for someone to recognize your talents or give you a break is frustrating for you and those around you. You miss out when you don't ask. Do any of these situations seem familiar?

- You've seen a promotion or your dream job handed to someone without your credentials or experience.
- A coworker is given opportunities to travel or be involved in a project you would love to do.
- You decide a person is too popular or good-looking to date someone like you. And that person ends up dating one of your nerdy friends.
- A friend receives a better hotel room or an upgraded airplane seat. You took what you were assigned.
- Someone else makes a major life decision for you without consulting you.

Not making requests works to your disadvantage in other ways too. When you repeatedly *consider* making a request and fail to ask, you send the message that you are satisfied. You signal that you're not ready to move forward right now. It's like preparing for a journey and stopping just steps away from your destination. Here's what some of the survey respondents said about their reluctance to ask.

*I wish I had the courage, but being told no cripples me.*

*Ninety percent of the time I'd rather go without than to ask for a favor.*

*I was taught to be happy with what I have.*

By not following through with your request, you never know for sure what is possible. And the people with authority to grant or deny your request have no idea of your preparation or desire to have something different. By not asking, you've removed that person's chance to consider your request and give you an answer.

## Asking is a brave act.

### What if you were brave?

Asking outrageously requires vulnerability and giving up some control. Sometimes you have to risk looking stupid or hearing the word "no." The best results come from minimizing the unknowns, structuring the elements you can control, and then simply having the courage to make your request.

If you are worn out from thinking about requests you don't make, tired of just accepting what you are given, and ready to improve your results, you might want to try asking for what you really do want.

## If I Were Brave

The lyrics from the song "If I Were Brave" by Jana Stanfield and Jimmy Scott describe the courage it takes to ask outside your comfort zone:

*What if we're all meant to do what we secretly dream?*
*What would you ask if you knew you could have anything?...*
*If I refuse to listen to the voice of fear*
*Would the voice of courage whisper in my ear*
*What would I do today if I were brave?*

You can download this song for free at AskOutrageously. com. (Reproduced by permission of Jana Stanfield and Jimmy Scott.)

### Top Ten Reasons to Ask Outrageously

1. **Shockingly good outcomes.** It's not unusual for people to ask for something they feel is outrageous and then report the person on the receiving end wasn't shocked at all by the request. Often the person asked is delighted to help or wondered why the request wasn't made sooner.
2. **Evidence of passion.** When you clearly show your interest, it is contagious. People will know you are engaged and invested in getting better results. By asking, you indicate that you know what you want, are ready for a change, and want to achieve big goals.
3. **Powerful appearance.** People who make bold requests improve their chances of being heard. By asking powerful questions, you improve your ability to influence and show confidence, no matter what the subject.

4. **Receive an answer.** By asking, you obtain a reply, even if it's "no" or "not yet." With an answer to your request, you can adjust, adapt, and move ahead. You can save time, resources, and mental effort. Most importantly, you stop wondering what could be if only you had the courage to ask.

5. **Build trust.** When you request what you want up front, people stop searching for your hidden agenda. Others want to help you more because they trust you more.

6. **Level the playing field.** Asking questions helps decrease any real or perceived power imbalances. Instead of accepting what is presented, asking questions lets people know you do your homework and are prepared to debate if needed.

7. **Avoid wasting time.** Asking allows you to avoid spending time with the wrong people. You'll quickly determine who can and will assist you in achieving the outcomes you want.

8. **Receive more than requested.** When you find the courage to ask outside your comfort zone, you discover the limitations you imagined aren't always real. Asking allows you to maximize the possibilities and gives you more options.

9. **Feel fantastic.** Perhaps the most remarkable result is how people feel after they ask. When you feel the fear and ask anyway, you gain confidence and a greater sense of worth.

10. **Earn respect.** People enjoy dealing with others who encourage them to think bigger. People with high potential want leadership models who successfully take risks, impact others, make effective decisions, and exceed expectations.

### Make Asking a Habit

Condition yourself to ask outside your comfort zone on a regular basis. Start with safe requests. Ask for more in your personal life and watch your results improve in business too. And get comfortable with the word "no." In fact, if you are not hearing no, you are probably not asking for enough. Keep asking until you get the no.

When you concentrate on making requests as a habit, asking becomes second nature. If you can become more comfortable asking everywhere, you'll ask when it really counts. In the heat of a big request, you will achieve results others can't conceive at the time. Stay open to receiving results that surpass your greatest expectations.

### Lead Others to Ask

Ask the people you are leading or coaching to take the free assessment "How Well Do You Ask?" (page 18) or online at AskOutrageously.com. Review the results of their assessment and the Top Ten Reasons to Ask Outrageously (page 26). Ask them, "Where would you like to focus on asking for more?" "What reasons resonated the most with you?" and "What results would be possible if asking became a habit?"

### Outrageous Review

- Simple questions in history have led to outrageous outcomes.
- Most people don't ask. They wish they had the nerve to ask for something big but don't ask or settle for something safe. They wait too long to ask and watch someone else ask and get what they really wanted. They feel stuck when it is time to move on or advance.

- There is a disconnect between why people think they are told no and why they are actually told no. The success of your request is not just about gathering more information, timing, and funds.
- Your precise word choice, fear of bothering someone, or looking foolish should not be your primary concerns.
- Improve your outcomes by focusing on the real reasons people are told no, which are 1) the request is inappropriate; and 2) the person being asked doesn't like, respect, or trust the person making the request.
- You can increase your wins and improve your results by asking outside your comfort zone. When you concentrate on making requests as a habit, asking becomes second nature.

 ### Smart Asks
- What would I ask for if I were brave?
- What am I unsatisfied with at work or home?
- When I fail to ask, what message am I sending?
- How can I develop trust and respect from the person I'm asking?

 ### Ask List
- If you haven't taken the assessment "How Well Do You Ask?" (page 18), please take it now. Then look at the results to determine your current skill level.
- Look through the "Top Ten Reasons to Ask Outrageously" (page 26). Identify the top two reasons that resonate with you.

 ### Secret Success Tools
Download the song "If I Were Brave" by Jana Stanfield and Jimmy Scott for free at AskOutrageously.com.

# Two

# Show Up Powerfully

Knowing how others view you is important when making powerful requests. Your family and your friends know the "real" you. However, when you are asking others, there is a good chance you are meeting for the first time.

A few brave souls can ask confidently without assigning much significance to being turned down or how others think of them. One out of five of the study participants reported they have no difficulties asking anyone for what they want. Here are some of their responses to asking outrageously.

*I have no problem asking for what I want in a business setting ... most people will answer anything I ask, even if it doesn't pertain to the specific request.*

*The worst response you can get is a no, so why not ask?*

*I know to start asking questions even if I'm not sure what the right question is. Opening the dialogue often takes me in unexpected directions and to answers I didn't know I wanted.*

## Master Requesters

You may live with a courageous asker. Often, family members, even very young ones, are convincing and tenacious. Think of children who really want a toy or a treat. Their ability to connect, stay the course, and ask questions is entertaining. The word "no" doesn't intimidate them. They concentrate on what they want and are persistent in their pursuit. Master requesters know requests are situational and can vary depending on the people and issues involved. They consider the best methods to relate to the person who has power and change their approach as needed. They are curious and very creative in asking an unlimited supply of questions. And they are successful more often than not.

Without reservation, they ask for a little more. They ask for better terms or greater outcomes. Observe them as they ask for information, favors, or special treatment. No one intimidates them. No request is too small or too large. They know the more they ask, the more they can learn or gain. While others are gathering unnecessary data or waiting for perfect conditions, master requesters make an initial request and move on to ask elsewhere.

Often their success in business can be tied to a willingness to ask for what others won't. They are respected. People are willing to answer their questions and go the extra mile to help them. Study the masters. Watch people who bravely make requests and follow their lead.

### How do you show up?

When you meet a stranger, what would be his or her initial impression of you? Your initial impression goes beyond how stylishly you're dressed or if your hair looks great that day. Do you portray confidence, trust, and approachability? Master requesters know exactly how they show up the first time. Through the years, they have listened to feedback and observed techniques

---

### Are You a Quest Master or a Master Requester?

Review your last few opportunities to ask. Determine if you are making requests or if you are stalling by taking unproductive quests. Signals you are questing include:

- Researching insignificant and unrelated issues.
- Waiting for a perfect time that never comes.
- Overpreparing and paralysis by analysis.
- Unrealistic worrying about someone's perception of you.
- Mentally reviewing unlikely scenarios, objections, or threats.
- Getting ready to get ready supported by unfounded excuses.

---

that work. These masters recognize when they appear intimidating and take action to lighten the conversation. They know if they seem young or inexperienced, and they choose whether to correct or use that perception. They make a conscious effort to be approachable and to help others feel comfortable.

### Approachability
Approachability goes beyond professional attire and a well-groomed look. An approachable person:

- Smiles and makes eye contact.
- Has a firm handshake and is polite.
- Helps others feel comfortable and heard.
- Develops an engaging presentation style.
- Consciously uses positive body language.
- Uses proper grammar, spelling, and language.
- Responds in a timely manner to emails, phone calls, and other communication.

## Traits of Master Requesters

- Approachable and considerate
- Perceptive and appropriate
- Positive and genuinely interested in others
- Respected and respectful
- Appreciative of others' efforts
- Flexible and adaptable

First impressions are made in thirty seconds or less. Spend more than thirty seconds getting ready for them.

### Nona

Nona's legal assistant scheduled an appointment with a new client. When business owner Bob Smith arrives for his appointment, Nona greets him warmly: "Hi, Mr. Smith. I'm Nona. Welcome. Let's go back to the conference room." Confused, Bob looks at Nona and asks, "Are you going to take me to see the employment attorney?" Nona smiles and laughingly responds, "Here I am." Bob, not smiling, says gruffly, "Young lady, I'm here about a serious business matter. I need to see someone with experience."

Nona may have some cultural biases working against her. She is a woman in what some consider a man's field and appears young. Nona didn't add to her credibility with her lighthearted introduction. She created the impression she was subservient by addressing Bob formally and introducing herself using only her first name. Bob may therefore doubt whether she has the required knowledge and experience to handle his issue.

To salvage this meeting, Nona isn't disrespectful, but she is assertive. "Bob, I have practiced law for six years. I am a partner and no one has more experience with employment matters at our firm. However, we do have lawyers who are older. If you prefer, we have an attorney in the office that is twenty years older than I am. While he doesn't have a background in employment law, he did pass the bar a few months ago. Which of us would you like to speak with today?" Bob wisely choses Nona; and Nona learned a big lesson in first impressions.

When you know you don't look the part, be strategic and know your stuff.

### *Joe*

Joe Solinski is successful asking potential clients to become immediate clients. "First impressions are important. I give prospects a history of our twenty-year-old company so they know we have the experience and expertise to do anything they need to get their properties in order." A seasoned presenter, Joe translates complicated situations into easily understood language for the non-engineering executives. He interjects humor to break the ice. Joe uses photographs to show his firm's creative solutions to challenging and complex construction problems.

Also a competitive bodybuilder and musician/singer, Joe is aware his appearance can be inconsistent with more conservative expectations. "I know I have long hair and don't look like most owners of commercial consulting firms, and that is certainly my choice. I have to be who I am in order to be the best I can be for our clients." Joe adds, "The most stern and challenging clients in the initial meetings are usually the ones that remain clients for life."

### Identify Your Strengths

Understanding the strengths you bring to the table is one of the first ways to increase your power when asking. People downplay their gifts and natural abilities. If you are approachable and naturally friendly, you may not count those traits as talents or strengths. Or if your gift is to understand complexities and numbers, you may wish for better presentation skills. Being well rounded is overrated. Being an expert at what you do well is how you get the most compensation. Concentrate on those strengths and develop them.

### Own Your Strengths

Determine two of your strengths and use them in a conversation with others at least three times. Here are some ideas you can use to fill in the blanks.

- My job here is to _____ and _____.
- I really enjoy _____ and _____.
- People depend on me to _____ and _____.
- Example: My job here is to think logically and to check our quality.

### *Adopt*

Think back. Have you been told you have a talent that you know you've never developed? For instance, has someone told you that you are confident or good at organizing? How did you respond to that compliment? Did you thank the person or internally question his or her observation? Maybe you know others, even relatives, who you think are much better at that skill. That person doesn't know that your big brother is the really confident one in the family or that your dad is the neat freak. People's evaluations of you are based on their experience of the community as a whole. The people who are complimenting you just know you.

## Identify Your Strengths and Talents

Look through the following list of characteristics or qualities. This is a small sampling of strengths and talents you may possess. Decide which apply to you.

- ☐ Adapt to change
- ☐ Analyze
- ☐ Coach
- ☐ Communicate
- ☐ Connect with others
- ☐ Contribute to a team
- ☐ Create
- ☐ Explain
- ☐ Facilitate discussions
- ☐ Influence others
- ☐ Initiate
- ☐ Innovate
- ☐ Lead
- ☐ Listen
- ☐ Make decisions
- ☐ Manage projects
- ☐ Manage risk
- ☐ Negotiate
- ☐ Present
- ☐ Resolve conflict
- ☐ Set goals and strategy
- ☐ Solve problems
- ☐ Support systems
- ☐ Troubleshoot
- ☐ Understand technical issues
- ☐ Others: _____

If people recognize a strength that would be helpful for you to possess, decide to adopt it. Start by observing people who have developed that talent and model your behavior after theirs. Use the language they use to ask and respond to questions. Observe how they manage stress or react when surprised. Ask yourself, "What would they request in this situation?" Then just ask as they would.

---

**If others are spotting a talent or characteristic, there is a strong likelihood you have it. Find ways to strengthen and develop those gifts.**

---

### *Adapt*

Have you heard words used to describe you that make you cringe? Before you try to eliminate or change that behavior, pause. Often, strengths that were undeveloped behavior when you were younger become valuable assets when you are older. Being bossy as a child can morph into being a leader who makes impactful decisions. The class clown becomes a master storyteller and marketing expert. The child who cries too easily grows into an empathetic adult with an intuition about angry customers or the best way to serve disaster victims. The youngster who took apart everything to see how it worked becomes an engineer or a business strategist.

Instead of dismissing a trait of yours, decide how that description could be upgraded or adapted to serve you better. When would that quality be great to have? What training do you need to make it a superpower? Watch strong people who use their similar characteristics or power for good. Adapt the positive aspects of the trait to serve you better. Rein in the less desirable aspects and upgrade the beneficial behavior. Keep those stronger descriptions in mind when you make requests.

## Strengthen Your First Impression

Are there any words describing you that you don't think are helpful or positive? Adapt or upgrade them to more powerful forms. Here are some examples.

| Initial/Undeveloped Behavior | Stronger/Upgraded Strength |
| --- | --- |
| Sweet | Kind and approachable |
| Talkative | Great communicator |
| Shy | Good listener and sensitive |
| Aggressive | Assertive and bold |
| Bossy | Decisive leader |
| Micromanager | Analytical and attentive to detail |
| Overly sensitive | Intuitive and caring |

You can draw confidence in possessing and optimizing your personal strengths.

### *Liesel*

Liesel knows the people in her company are more detail oriented than she is. She is better at forming relationships and communicating but doesn't see much value in her own strengths. Her perception changes when the group discusses developing client relationships. Liesel quickly sees that the ideas the group is proposing are not going to work. "Instead of a technical newsletter, which most people will consider spam, could we try something that will connect us with our potential clients?" Liesel asks. Then she gives five powerful ideas to communicate and build relationships. Weeks later, Liesel overhears some company leaders saying, "You know, this is more Liesel's area. She's so strong in relationships and communication. Let's go ask her opinion."

You have talents and strengths you easily command that others marvel at and wish they possessed. Own those gifts and develop them. They help you show up powerfully and give you secret confidence whenever you ask for anything.

## Strategies to Convey Confidence

You've seen people walk in with confidence. The ability to show up powerfully and command attention develops over time. Here are strategies you can practice.

**Pretend you are hosting, instead of attending, your next party or reception.** Think about actions a host takes to make others feel welcome. For instance, a host asks people about their work and hobbies. A host connects people with introductions and shares areas or topics in which they have common experience or interest.

**Determine if you should be formal or more familiar in your approach.** In some communities, regions, and countries, using formal titles is important. If you are unsure of the local custom, there is a workaround: Use both first and last names. Instead of saying "Mr. South, I'm Kelly," say, "Jim South, I'm Kelly Vasquez." If you are introducing others for the first time, try "Jane North, I'm Bae Park, and this is Roberto Flores." Also, if you can't determine how to address someone, you can *ask* him or her.

**When making presentations, remind yourself that the information you are presenting is extremely important.** You are there to have a conversation and make sure the attendees understand the most important points. Stop worrying if you appear as a runway model or sound like a vocal artist. When your key concern is that participants fully grasp the messages they need, any pictures, stories, slides, and supporting materials are simply there to support those messages.

**If you aren't being heard or acknowledged when you are in a meeting, stand up.** Your voice power will increase and your energy will too. Also, it's difficult to ignore a person standing while everyone else is seated. If available, walk over to a whiteboard or flip chart while you are up and diagram your points for visual emphasis *and* to support the reason you are standing (versus potentially appearing to be aggressive).

### Lina

Lina dreads the monthly meeting with the team. There is no real agenda and the loudest voices get heard. Also, everyone is so poised, so quick-witted and put together. She always feels less shiny and far less clever in the midst of these brilliant people. Today, Lina needs the team to listen to a critical initiative. She waits for a lull in the conversation, abruptly stands up, and asks, "Has everyone heard of the initiative to add more military veterans to our workforce? The change will affect our government contracts, our recruiting efforts, and our performance objectives." Once she has their attention, Lina distributes supporting documents and begins discussing her ideas.

**Mimic the body language of the most powerful people you know.** They stand up straight, make appropriate eye contact, and use gestures to convey their points. Look at their feet. Usually they are placed about shoulder-width apart. They have an open stance. They smile and nod when they agree.

**Ask questions.** Top decision makers ask a multitude of questions to understand what's going on and determine what should happen next. People don't think they are ill-informed or wasting their time. The opposite is true. You should ask questions too.

---

## It's courageous to ask outrageous!

---

### Build Courage

One of the biggest confidence builders is seeing the power of making requests. When you don't know how to approach a request, use these strategies to get unstuck.

**Ask the advice of a child.** When you have no clue how to make a request, talk to children or teens. Generally, you'll be surprised at the questions they ask and the appropriateness of their advice. In addition, the act of simplifying your request to its fundamental elements has value when you communicate your request later.

**Imagine a board of directors.** *Mentally* assemble experts on the topics you are requesting. When you want assistance making requests about managing employees, think about what the best bosses and leaders would do in your situation. Do you have a business finance question? Think of the questions the smartest financial minds would pose. Mentally keep these experts in reserve to use as examples to follow.

**Become the adviser.** When you are asking, pretend you are an advisor or consultant solving a problem. The request is no longer about you. The preparation and questions you ask should revolve around the issue faced.

**Pretend that you have already made the request.** Pay attention to your thoughts and how your body feels or reacts. If you have regrets or worry about the repercussions, you may not be ready to ask. Feeling relieved and relaxed are good signs you are on the right track.

Determine the request you would make if you knew you couldn't lose or fail. Now, identify those areas that might cause you to get off track. Then ask yourself, "How would I address those detours and how likely are those areas to appear?"

With some insight, a little practice, and focus, you can adopt confidence when asking for anything, including personal requests. You can increase your chance of being heard and respected. To improve your results and get more of what you really want, start examining your first impression and compare yourself with master requesters.

 ## Lead Others to Ask

Ask the people you lead and coach to choose three to five of the strengths and talents that describe them on the list on page 37. Compare their choices with what you would have chosen. Discuss your selections and insights. Then ask them:

- "How could you develop this strength?"
- "Where could you use more of this talent at work?"
- "What support do you need from me?"
- "How could you use this strength to make more effective requests?"

### Outrageous Review

- The first step to asking outrageously is to show up powerfully.
- Observe others and note your first impression of them.
- Pay attention to how people perceive you.
- Be intentional about being approachable.
- To build your confidence, know your own strengths and talents. Identifying your strengths isn't bragging, just as asking for what you want isn't being greedy.

- Outrageous is courageous. Asking is a brave act. Push through fear that stems from past mistakes or not knowing what response you will receive.

## Smart Asks

- What am I good at doing?
- What do I notice about people who make a good first impression?
- How can I be more approachable?
- What is a trait that people see in me that I could adopt or adapt?

## Ask List

- Ask for help in identifying your strengths and talents.
- Give the list of possible talents in this chapter (see Identify Strengths and Talents) to three people.
- Ask them to select five strengths or talents that apply to you and then send you the results.
- Practice the Strategies to Convey Confidence and the Strategies to Build Courage.

## Secret Success Tool

If you'd like a form with wording to help you with this challenge, go to AskOutrageously.com and download the tool Identify Strengths and Talents.

Three

# The Right Focus

To ask powerfully and outrageously, you have to clearly request what you want. Other people are busy and concerned with their own needs. You must be your own advocate and clearly ask for what you want. You can't hint. You can't hope someone spots your good efforts. You can't make statements with the expectation that others will pick up on your signals or decipher your code or hidden message.

Place the right attention on communicating and connecting with others, and watch your requests and outcomes improve. Nothing else you attempt will generate breakthrough results like these two recommendations:

1. Ask for *what* you really want.
2. Focus on the *person* who can help you get it.

### Focus on What You Really Want

You are busy and your time is valuable. Why waste your efforts? Determine in advance what you want and why. Clarity improves your ability to articulate your objective and achieve it. Before making any request, big or small, ask yourself:

- What do I want?
- What are the good reasons?
- Is the work involved worth my time and effort?
- Is the outcome I want appropriate and available?

What do you want? *Really?*

Be crystal clear about the outcome you want to reach with your request. Know what constitutes a win or outrageous outcome and what is acceptable if you need to compromise. When you define your goal, you can monitor how close you are to achieving it. Without clarity, you can flounder and not realize whether you should quit or continue.

---

**Too many opportunities are lost because people didn't know when to stop. Don't keep asking for more when you've already won more than you requested.**

---

People censor what they ask for because they see the request as too much or in the extreme. Some don't ask because they don't want to be vulnerable or can't control the outcome. They limit or stop themselves when an opportunity goes beyond what they planned or can conceive. Don't block yourself by thinking "this person will never do that" or "I'd never give someone that." This self-monitoring keeps you from getting the deals you could.

### Get Over Yourself

Remember when you were a teenager? Your parents told you, "The world does not revolve around you. It is not all about you." Turns out, they were right.

According to Suzanne Livingston, certified master coach, people often subconsciously hold themselves back from asking

## Dead-End Questions That Get You Nowhere

People can undermine results by placing too much attention on themselves. Don't concentrate on immaterial nonsense. Which of these questions have you asked yourself?

- Should I ask for something that big?
- What if I make a mistake or things get worse?
- Should I just wait?
- What if I look stupid?
- If they say no, will it hurt my reputation?
- Would it be better for someone else to make this request instead of me?
- What would someone else (my mom, dad, brother, sister, kids, spouse, neighbors, boss, peers, coworkers, employees, or dead great uncle) say about my asking this?

Questions like these send you on unnecessary detours and place roadblocks in your path to improving your results. Stop asking them.

for what they really want. "Impression management" often hinders people from asking. Suzanne says,

> We are taught from an early age that being acceptable, proper, or viewed as "good" in the eyes of our caretakers, authority figures, and communities is more important than what we may want most. For adults, impression management is usually subconscious and automatic, and we don't always know it's running the show.

Research proves that no matter how much time, money, or energy you invest in improving yourself, *it will never be enough.* You can spend a fortune on looking and sounding the best. You can build your expertise and increase your experience. You can prepare to respond to any objection, denial, or rejection.

---

### Your pursuit of being perfect won't help you receive the results you want.

---

Are you concerned how someone might perceive you when you ask? You don't have time to spend in fruitless attempts at achieving perfection or managing your image. Instead, concentrate on how the request affects the person you are asking.

### Prepare to Ask Boldly

Focus on asking for what you really want—no second-guessing, no wondering how you appear. How do you decide if you are asking for enough?

- Ask yourself what has worked for you in the past and if that approach is worth trying with this request.
- Ask your peers, boss, friends, and family what or how they attempted or requested in similar circumstances.
- Ask yourself what you could offer that the other party would value. Identify options that are easy and inexpensive.
- Ask yourself what you could request that would be easy and inexpensive for the other party to provide.

### *Name your request*

What's in a name? Naming your request mentally separates your ask from you as an individual and helps you think more objectively. For instance, you could name your request "Operation Request Time Off" or "Ask to Attend the California Training." If your request is denied, the denial isn't a personal rejection of you. Instead, this particular request with these particular facts on this particular day was turned down.

---

### Focus Your Ask

You improve your focus by writing down or verbalizing your desired outcome. Once you reach your destination, you can feel comfortable with reaching a stopping point or being satisfied with the outcome. Fill in the blanks:

My outrageous ask is to: _____
_____

Examples: Ask for a raise that reflects the effort I've shown. Have a particular employee show up on time and do her job. Get my teen to honor his curfew.

The good reasons I want this goal are:
_____
_____

Outrageous outcome: I know I've obtained my request when:
_____
_____

---

### Your good reasons

Be able to support your requests with good reasons. Many times, asking on its own is enough. However, you'll be surprised how many people are willing to help you reach your objectives if you tell them your rationale for wanting to achieve those objectives.

According to the Ask Outrageously Study, people don't want to inconvenience others. Are you prepared to hear the number one request that people won't make? Respondents overwhelmingly agreed: *they won't ask to cut in line.*

According to the study, 52 percent would *never* ask. People reported that they would rather borrow money than ask to cut in line!

What's so scary about asking to cut in line? You would let someone go ahead of you to check out, especially if you had a cart full of items and that person had two items. In fact, other research studies show people are more than willing to let you cut in line, especially if you give them a reason when you ask.

### Just because

As a child you learned that "please" and "thank you" are considered magic words. In asking, add another word to the magic category: "because." One study showed that people increased the likelihood of hearing yes when they used the word "because" after the request. When a person asked to cut in line to make copies, people said yes 60 percent of the time. However, when the same person asked, "May I cut in line *because* ...," people said yes 94 percent of the time. The reason following the word "because" didn't matter. Whether it was "because I'm in a rush" or, ridiculously, "because I need to make copies," both statements increased the percentage of people granting the request. (This study of quick requests involving small decisions was originally performed in the 1970s by psychologist Ellen Langer and was replicated as recently as 2009 by Scott Key and colleagues at Northern Illinois University and Union College.)

### Is it worth it to you?

Making asking a habit is key to asking outrageously. However, not everything that can be requested *should* be requested. Your time and energy are limited. Determine what is easy or what could have a big impact. If your request has been rejected several times, don't invest your time on it any longer. If you decide your odds of your request being granted are slim or not worth the consequences, ask for something more appropriate or available.

**Lead Others to Ask**

Ask your people to complete a Focus Your Ask Form (page 49) and run through the request with you. Ask them to role-play with you. Allow them to play the people they are asking and you play the requester. (Switching roles allows them to see how you ask and respond to objections they anticipate.)

**Outrageous Review**

- You must be your own advocate and clearly ask for what you want. Don't hint or hope someone spots your efforts.
- Impression management or "what they might think of me" may be holding you back from asking for what you want. Remember, that discomfort was there to help you as a child but doesn't have to dictate your life as an adult. It's safe to be bold. Ask for what you want.
- Be crystal clear about your desired outcomes when making requests. Know what a win is for you.
- There's a difference between success and perfection. When asking, your goal is success (getting a yes), not perfection. Don't stall by trying to make your request perfect.
- Let people you are asking decide how to answer you. Don't shy away from asking because (you think) you know what their answer will be.
- Avoid "what if" thoughts that question your reasons.

 **Smart Asks**

- Is this request worth it to me?
- What do I really want?
- What are my good reasons?
- Is what I'm seeking appropriate and available?
- If the worst thing happens when I make a request, what will I do?

### Ask List

- Ask if you can cut in front of a person with an overflowing grocery cart using "because" with a reason.
- Complete the Focus Your Ask Form (page 49) for a request in the next week.

### Secret Success Tools

If you'd like a form with wording to help you with this challenge, go to AskOutrageously.com and download the tool Focus Your Ask Form.

# Four

# What's in It for Them?

You can prepare your request in great detail but fail to consider benefits for the other party. Ignoring their interests creates unnecessary obstacles. You waste time and energy in making your request and arguing for your position. People are less willing to listen to others who haven't acknowledged their needs or realized their limitations.

Keep in mind that everyone is concentrating on his or her own interests. *Everyone.* Have you heard of WII-FM, or "What's in it—for me?" Instead of concentrating on your own needs, train yourself to revise your request to consider the needs of others. Ask yourself WII–FT, "What's in it—for them?" Realize the limits the other side may face. No matter how persuasive or likeable you are, no one is going to jeopardize his or her job or risk professional embarrassment to grant your request.

The Ask Outrageously Study findings show most people are working too hard on areas that don't help and won't matter (see Figure 5). The number one way people feel confident when asking for what they want is if they "know the details and have done their research." Yes, *details* and *research.* Change that focus to consider others' objectives and reasons.

### The I's Don't Have It

If you want to be heard, take the focus off yourself. When considering other people's interests, ask:

- Would this request put them in a better position?
- How will saying yes to me benefit them?
- What can I do to make sure they feel listened to?
- How can I show them I respect their opinions?
- How would people know without a doubt that I am looking out for their best interests as well as my own?
- How do I show I am willing to adapt or be flexible?

## Is It Worth It to Them?

Your answers to the list of questions in the section Focus on *What* You Really Want (see page 45) helped you determine your must-haves, or essentials. Now consider how others might view your request. To make your request valuable to them, ask and answer the same questions. Think about all the stakeholders involved, and then ask:

- What do they want?
- What are their good reasons?
- Is this worth their time and effort?
- Is *what* they want appropriate and available?

Attempting to answer these questions will help you think creatively and identify the good reasons others may want to help you. Also, you can determine how committed the other side might be to granting your request. If you can't determine *why* it is worth the other person's time and effort, ask the person what would make it worth his or her while.

**Figure 5**
**When I ask for something, I feel more confident when I ...**

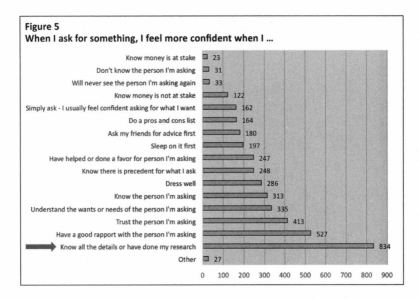

Many people grant requests if you just ask them. People have their own reasons for helping you. Your request may require a little effort or it may simply be something they do regularly. They may like the feeling of helping others. They may appreciate your business or want to gain you as a customer. You may remind them of someone they like, including themselves.

### Socheata

Filmmaker Socheata Poeuv grew up in the United States never knowing that her family had survived the Khmer Rouge genocide. She and her husband created their independent film, *New Year Baby*, to tell her story. They needed an animator to create a short piece to depict a portion of Cambodian history. As new film graduates, they couldn't afford the cost, which would be several hundred thousand dollars. Because the animator liked the concept and they *asked*, he did the piece for a fraction of the cost. When they first started talking, they could not have known that the animator had a personal reason for helping them with their project: he was also a refugee.

You are limited to the information available to you. You can't know for certain *why* people choose to act one way or precisely *what* they want. Your perception of what another person might think, feel, say, or do is incomplete. You aren't a mind reader.

---

## Their reasons are their reasons.

---

### Ask Them What They Want

Although it helps to know other people's motivators, all is not lost if you don't know. You may never know why people say yes or no. Don't waste time attempting to pinpoint why they help you. If you got your yes, that's a good time to stop, thank them, and move on. Don't give people who grant your request a reason to change their minds.

The same things that motivate you do not necessarily motivate other people. Their needs, wants, and desires may well differ from yours. *Reflect on your personal relationships if you need proof.* Whether their reasons are logical or you understand them, people have their own explanations and reasons.

### *What people value*

Consider what others may want. It is astonishingly easy to create value that others want and to strengthen agreements. Parties often underestimate the value of items or services they can offer. You probably have information or services considered very valuable to other people that costs you little or nothing to provide. Whether you offer support when they use a product, intelligence on who may need their help, or even a convenience like storing purchased equipment at your warehouse until a new building is ready, you may have something they want and value and that you would be happy to provide. *Ask them.*

### *Kerry*

A managing director of professional development, Kerry asks her vice president to provide funding for a facilitator to teach a course her department will be offering. He says yes to cover most of the cost. Now two of her staff can see the material presented and then certify online. Pleased at training more people without the inconvenience or cost. Kerry says, "This request saved us travel expenses as well as time away from the office. What a deal!"

### Easy Asks

People may be willing to give you valuable items, services, or information for free or at a discounted cost. *Ask them.* And to improve the results you receive, consider what costs little for *them* to provide that you value. Then request or suggest those resources.

*My neighbor said he won a new iPad, and that he didn't have much use for his old one. This was low-hanging fruit. I asked for it. Now I have my own iPad and I don't have to share it with my husband.*

## Make your request easy to say yes to.

### *Wendel*

Board Certified in Civil Trial Law and Personal Injury Trial Law, Wendel Withrow has a different approach from that of many lawyers. He helps the opposing parties do their job.

Wendel communicates regularly with adjusters and opposing counsel to update them on his clients' status. He even forwards medical records, police reports, and other documents at no cost, which saves them the time, trouble, and expense of acquiring them formally. Wendel says, "Why not make it easier and quicker for the other side to see you have a clear case up front? When I call and ask to resolve cases, they are informed and have what they need to make a decision. If we can't settle, we can always go to trial."

---

**Look for the low-hanging fruit. It's easier to reach and doesn't require a ladder.**

---

The notion you must work extremely hard or don't deserve what little you receive can stifle making requests. If your success doesn't seem real because you didn't work hard to acquire it, get over it. Not everything has to be hard won or a difficult challenge.

*When my son found the condo he liked, I offhandedly said to the salesperson, "It's too bad I can't get my broker's commission on this." She said, "You can!"*

### Kris

Kris Harrison is the CEO of a Saudi Arabian startup that provides clients with solutions in telecommunications. Kris saw his opportunity while looking for new office space in downtown Riyadh. When Kris discovered that the existing tenant was moving to larger offices, he made his request. "I outrageously asked him to take $5,000 for all existing office furniture on site. I suggested that he could simply pack up the company's personal belongings and laptops and move to the new office without the hassle of moving or taking the trouble to sell the items.

"Bingo! Agreement made. We moved into a ready-made office two weeks later. As a new startup, we had zero furnishings. The existing furniture, desks, chairs, and printers were less than one year old and in perfect condition. Asking saved me at least two months of operational costs."

Avoid creating additional work for others. For instance, don't make others interpret what you are asking. Clearly state your objective and the rationale supporting your request. Although you want to stay flexible about *how* your request is granted, providing *what* and the reasons *why* is your responsibility.

*I find that asking others to do something specific usually produces results. Asking someone to act on a concept by figuring out a good way to make it happen usually doesn't work. People are willing to perform tasks but are not as willing to assume responsibility for independent thinking and planning.*

Help people be good advocates for you. Make it easy for them to grant your request. Assist the other side in "selling" or explaining your request to others by asking, "What information would help you communicate this request?" Even people with high levels of authority need good reasons to justify their actions to others.

### Helen

Helen approaches her boss Karolina about working from home: "Karolina, can I start working from home three days a week? I know others do. Working at home would help me with my kids and in looking after my parents." Karolina responds, "I'd like to say yes. However, I'm not hearing any reasons why I should or how your request benefits the company. If you can think of some good reasons, let me know."

Helen returns later with an upgraded request. "Karolina, there are some good business reasons for me to have a home office. With all the meetings I attend on Mondays and Tuesdays, I never sit at my desk. I could make those my office days and free up needed work space. If I work from home, I'll be more available for conference calls in different time zones. Also, our client's north location is only five minutes from my house. I could visit there more frequently to troubleshoot and handle problems faster. Can you support my working from home?"

Karolina smiles. "I knew you would figure it out if I gave you a little time to think. Of course I'm willing. Now I have a good argument when my boss asks me why your request is good for our company." Although Helen asks outside her comfort zone, her request isn't groundbreaking. By requiring Helen to work through the rationale, Karolina helped her understand how to create appropriate business requests in the future.

### Shelby

Shelby is frustrated with her team's execution on a project. She asks her boss to intervene and force them to cooperate. Instead of agreeing, her boss replies, "Shelby, I've stepped in before and it isn't productive. It's your job to coordinate and connect in a productive way with the other departments. If you want to bring me ideas or options, I'll be more than happy to help you think through them." The next time Shelby returns for advice from the boss, she knows to ask for appropriate assistance but not expect to have her job done for her.

### Stop tweaking

Questions can dramatically change the help and performance you receive from others. People are more motivated and your job gets easier. Can you ask about their thinking or any areas of concern *without* giving them the answers? By asking questions you encourage others to solve problems and buy in to working on solutions. Let others phrase and support requests with good business reasons.

### Captain Abrashoff

Captain D. Michael Abrashoff, former commander of the USS *Benfold* and author of *It's Your Ship: Management Techniques from the Best Damn Ship in the Navy*, asked crew members about their lives, their upbringing, their future plans, and their motivation for joining the Navy. One at a time, he asked about their roles on *Benfold*. What did they like most? Least? What would they change if they could?

Asking questions created outrageous results. In 1998, the ship operated on 75 percent of its allocated budget. Captain Abrashoff said, "Sailors were free to question conventional wisdom and dream up better ways to do their jobs.... As a result, we returned $600,000 of the ship's $2.4 million maintenance budget and $800,000 of its $3 million repair budget." They set Navy records *and* they re-enlisted. Abrashoff says, "Even I find this startling, but the numbers don't lie. The ship's retention rate for the two most critical categories jumped from 28 percent to 100 percent, and stayed there."

Rein in the tweaking or adjusting when you say yes as well. An unequivocal yes without any exceptions is much more engaging.

"Look for an immediate opportunity to give a yes without a condition or constraint," suggests Pamela Jett, author of *Com-*

*municate to Keep 'Em: Enhancing Employee Engagement through Remarkable Communication.* "These yeses sound like:

- Yes, go for it!
- I like it. Make it happen.
- Great idea. Let's do it.

Say yes with no conditions, no added value, no tweaks or adjustments. A yes that says you trust employee or team."

---

## Stop going for right ... go for right now.

---

### Timing

How do you handle the timing of a request? Do you ask whenever the thought strikes you? If so, you may not be prepared to support your request. Are you waiting because you don't want to be a nuisance? Do you worry you'll be viewed less favorably if you ask? If you are prepared, the best time to ask could be right now. You can pre-empt your requests unnecessarily. Waiting to ask can mean you miss your opportunity altogether.

*Everyone's day is filled. I find it hard to get time just to make the ask.*

*People have so much on their plates these days. My concern is whether the benefit of their time and effort overrules me just doing it myself.*

### Margo

Margo and her colleague are sharing a room for a business conference that will last five days. When booking the room, they requested a view of the ocean. Upon arrival, though, they receive a room with a not-so-beautiful view of the roof and air conditioning unit. Margo reaches for the phone to talk to the front desk and ask for a better room. However, her colleague says, "Let's not bother them. This is probably the best room they have available, and we could get something worse." Margo replies that she's willing to risk it. She asks for another room and politely explains the original reservation. The front desk clerk checks the room availability and upgrades them to a nicer room with a view.

### Paula

At a silent auction fundraiser, Paula wanders over to the potted plants in ceramic containers. The plant in the blue container would look great in her office lobby. She wants to ask the person organizing the sale how she can buy the plant, but he looks busy. Paula doesn't want to bother him. As she waits, she sees a man pick the plant she wants and ask the organizer a question. He pulls out twenty dollars and walks off with *her* lobby plant. Paula sees one more plant she likes. This time, she pulls out her wallet, walks over to the organizer, and says, "Excuse me, I'd like to buy this plant."

### Time to wait

At times, you may not need to make a request at all. Many problems solve themselves over time without effort or a request on your part. Or it may be better to postpone your request until the person you'll be asking is calmer and can give you his or her undivided attention. Use these questions to determine the right time.

- Knowing what I know, if I wait for a "better" time, will that time ever come? (Is this person always busy? Is this as busy a time as any?)

- Realistically, will my chances for a favorable response improve or decrease by waiting?
- What questions can I ask to determine the right time?
- If someone made this request of me, could I respond now?
- If I don't ask now, when exactly will I make my request?

### Nate

Nate hates interrupting, but he needs William's advice on several matters. In the past when Nate knocked on the door, William sighed and said, "Yes? Can it wait?… I'm really under a time crunch here." Nate knows his upcoming requests will require William's full attention. So he asks, "William, can you meet this week to answer questions regarding three of our major clients? We'll need fifteen minutes of uninterrupted time. When can we meet and talk undisturbed?"

Busy, stressed people can explode at interruptions. At the time, you don't know if they are angry with you, annoyed at the interruption, or something else. Attempting to determine exactly what bothers others is rarely a good use of *your* time. Instead, save your ask for another day.

### Time to talk

Timing telephone conversations can be tough. Even if you reach the person and not voice mail, you have no visual cues. You aren't sure if you are interrupting or who is in the room. You are relying only on what the person says and the sound of his or her voice. You may choose to ask, "Is this a good time to talk?"—but beware of giving him or her the chance to avoid the conversation. You may need to be bold.

*Roger*

Roger, a financial adviser, is introduced by email to Kim. Thinking she has an important financial concern, Roger calls Kim first thing Monday morning. However, when Kim answers, she is curt and sounds stressed. Kim briskly says she is busy and doesn't have time to talk to Roger for several months. Roger hangs up feeling confused.

No one knows why Kim responded to Roger the way she did. Perhaps Kim was in a meeting, was caught off guard, was having an extremely stressful day, or wanted Roger to respond by email instead of calling. Roger sends a short email to Kim. He writes, "Kim, sounds like I caught you at a busy time. I'll call in six weeks. If you need me before then, please contact me." He copies his friend on the email and thanks him for the introduction. After receiving Roger's email, which jars her memory, a less-stressed Kim calls, apologizes, and sets up an appointment in two weeks.

Asking people when they want to meet and for how long creates a contract with them. Honor your side of the agreement by being timely and wrapping up when you say you will. Showing that you can meet your agreement about time helps you later when you make other requests.

### Deadlines

Short deadlines are often used to force people to make quick decisions or act on impulse. You've seen the "act now or lose" advertisements. Always ask first for more time. And be suspicious of people who won't grant you the time to consider.

*Jorge*

It's late at the dealership. When the new car is pulled to the front, Jorge looks at it closely. Something isn't right. "OK, if you'll just sign here, we can all go home," the salesperson says, looking at the time. Jorge honors his gut feeling and responds, "Before I can buy this car, I'm going to need five or ten minutes to review the paperwork and my research. Would you prefer that I come back in the morning? I know it's late."

The chance he might lose a sale brings the salesperson to attention. He tells Jorge to take the time he needs. When Jorge reviews his research on the car, he realizes what is wrong. The car advertised is not the same model as the one he researched or the one he test-drove. In addition, the upgrades are missing on this version of the vehicle. The switch is probably an honest mistake by a tired salesperson. Thankfully, Jorge's request of extra time to review his facts ensures he drives home in the right vehicle.

When you face a short deadline or the time you think you have is shortened, request an extension of time *first*, before you do anything else.

### Aaron

When Aaron arrives early to the meeting, everyone has coffee and is already in discussions. Feeling as if he's interrupted them, he double-checks his calendar and the agenda on his phone. No, he is definitely in the right room and early. The leader says, "We are ready for your presentation now." Aaron quickly fumbles to connect his computer and begin. Midway through the first few minutes, he is interrupted and is asked, "So, Aaron, what's the bottom line here? What do you want us to do?"

Knowing the group is ready to move on, Aaron fights the temptation to rush or leave. Instead he stops and poses a question. "There are three key points you need to hear that will take five to ten minutes depending on your questions. How would you like to proceed?" The group agrees to an additional ten minutes and the mood shifts from harried to respectful.

## Is the Request Appropriate and Available?

Have you ever spent hours preparing for something that wasn't available? Wasting resources and even chasing an unobtainable outcome is common. For instance, people can be involved in a lawsuit for years and not know what result they really want. Many times, the parties involved are asking for a desired result that cannot be addressed by the court system. People waste hours, weeks, or even months pursuing a process that doesn't get them what they want. The resolution they seek isn't available, so their requests are not appropriate.

### Dr. Smith and Dr. Wesson

Former partners in a medical practice, Dr. Smith and Dr. Wesson are attempting mediation to see if they can settle their lawsuit before trial. Dr. Wesson comes prepared with several flipchart posters showing reasons he is "right" and should win. The mediator looks at the posters and listens to Dr. Wesson's detailed explanation, then asks him a question: "Dr. Wesson, it sounds like you're asking for respect and would like an apology. What you are asking for is something a court can't force Dr. Smith to give you." Dr. Wesson realizes that he hasn't considered what "winning" would mean legally. Any money award would be eaten up by attorney's fees. Immediately, there is a shift in communication. Dr. Wesson asks to meet with Dr. Smith. The physicians talk about the events and even apologize to each other. Together they create a solution a court could not have awarded.

---

### You can disagree without being disagreeable.

---

#### Ridiculous requests

Requests may look ridiculous until you understand the reasoning for them. Have you heard about the outrageous request that led a jury to award $2.86 million from McDonald's to a woman who spilled coffee? What could lead an attorney to ask for and a jury to award such high damages for coffee a seventy-nine-year-old woman spilled on herself? Reviewing the facts of the case may help.

Plaintiff Stella Liebeck was injured with third-degree burns over 17 percent of her body and continued medical treatment for two years. She spent eight days in the hospital and received skin grafts. Also, McDonald's admitted that hundreds of people had been burned by its coffee. Where did the large amount of money come from? The plaintiff's attorney asked the jury to award one or two days of the company's coffee revenue to send a message to McDonald's to serve the coffee at a safer temperature.

Remember the outrageous request in which the rock band Van Halen demanded that no brown M&Ms be allowed backstage during their concerts? What would prompt the band to make such a ridiculous request to specify the color of M&Ms? The reason for the clause: the band wanted to make sure that promoters read and complied with the entire agreement and its detailed requirements. Seeing brown M&Ms alerted the band to pay closer attention to details, especially regarding stage weight requirements and safety. One such weight failure had caused $80,000 in damage when equipment sank through the stage.

Before you dismiss people who are asking for something you don't think is appropriate, ask how they arrived at their requests. The rationale might change your response. When you ask, focus on making requests that are appropriate and can be granted by the person you are asking. When you think you might surprise the person you ask, come prepared to educate and to discuss your reasoning.

### Lead Others to Ask

When you can easily see a solution, it is difficult not to offer direction or try to control the process. Instead, ask for solutions from each of the people you lead or coach. If at all possible, say "yes" or ask them to support the request or solution without editing or tweaking.

Ask your people to make their presentation for you and then practice summing up their requests in a few sentences. Listen to make sure that their messages are short with a clear call to action. With poor meeting management, speakers running over time, and emergencies, you never know when a meeting or presentation time will be reduced.

### Outrageous Review

- When you ask, the request is about something *you* want. Keep in mind that everyone is concentrating on his or her own interests.
- In most requests, people are thinking WII-FM, or "What's in it—for me." When asking, reframe your request to also address WII-FT, or "What's in it—for them." How your request benefits the other party may not be obvious to that person. You may need to bridge the gap.
- Sometimes you learn another person's reasons for granting your requests. Sometimes you don't. Sometimes the person doesn't know. Sometimes it's just "because."
- Create a scenario in which it's easy to say yes to you. Avoid creating additional work for others. Ask specifically for

what you want rather than ask someone to act on a concept and force him or her to figure out how to make your request happen.

## Smart Asks

- What do they want?
- What are their good reasons?
- Is this worth their time and effort?
- Is *what* they want appropriate and available?
- How can I make it easy for someone to say yes to my request?

## Ask List

- Look at your next presentation and see if you can get to the bottom line in one minute or less.
- In your next request, ask someone what he or she wants first *before* you ask for what you want.

## Secret Success Tools

Download the Outrageous Request Form from AskOutrageously.com.

# Five

# Trust and Respect

Relationships built on trust and respect increase outcomes for all involved. When you are honest in your efforts to compromise and are creative in your attempts to find a fair solution, others involved will reveal results you weren't aware were available. Find out the other person's true interests before you make a request based on your interests.

## Trust Factor

Few people have high trust factors built into their demeanor. Based on the initial impression they make, these lucky individuals possess the ability to connect quickly. Whether they learned the behavior or were born with it, they put others at ease just with their presence. What a gift to walk into a room confidently knowing people there perceive you as trustworthy, respectable, and approachable.

People frequently overlook the significance of trust in relationships when preparing to ask. In the Ask Outrageously Study, almost a third of respondents said they would deny a request or tell others no when they don't like, respect, or trust them (see page 23).

Do you naturally trust everyone you meet? You probably don't. Most people don't feel at ease or completely safe with someone new until they prove to be trustworthy. If others don't trust you, bad results occur. Decisions you make are questioned. At work, you are micromanaged or left out of important discussions. Even though you ask politely, you aren't given the information you need. At home, trust is even more important because it builds and sustains relationships.

### Troy

Troy is playing miniature golf with his son. For some reason, the windmill hole really got him today. When he writes down his score, his son asks, "Dad, why did you put down only three for this hole? You hit that ball eight times."

---

### Building Trust

You can build your trust factor and improve how others view you. Review the following list. Are there two areas where you could take action to accelerate building trust?

- Tell the truth and do what you say you will.
- Honor confidences and protect trade secrets.
- Don't cheat (even if no one would know about it).
- Seek help when you can't do it alone.
- Resist talking negatively about others.
- Accept responsibility and avoid placing blame.
- Stop harassment and bullying.
- Resist overcharging or taking advantage of others.
- Do the right thing, even if it costs you.
- Be on time.

## Manners Matter

Be polite. It turns out your momma was right. Good manners *are* important. In our study, a third of respondents said they are more likely to say no to a request if the person is inconsiderate or has bad manners. The advice seems so basic, yet not everyone follows it. Here's why being polite pays off:

- You show you are in control of your emotions.
- You give an example of how you want to be treated.
- Your words can't be used against you later.
- It pleasantly surprises others.
- You show others that you see them as people.
- You distinguish yourself from others.
- It's a sign of good upbringing and class.

"We need to pick our heads up from our electronic devices and go back to face-to-face communication and to remember the simple 'thank you' and 'you're welcome,'" notes Colleen Rickenbacher, author of *Be on Your Best Business Behavior*. The rule of reciprocity reinforces this point: "We should try to repay, in kind, what another person has provided us," says Robert B. Cialdini, author of *Influence: The Psychology of Persuasion and Pre-suasion*.

### Be nice

Being nice is a sign of strength, not weakness. Although it may take longer, being the nice guy or gal making a request usually gains you more trust, information, and commitment.

---

*As someone who grew up in the Bronx, I certainly learned my share of four-letter words, but none are more powerful than "nice."* — Linda Kaplan Thaler

---

*Ross*

Instead of just dropping off the documents at the townhome management office, Ross checks in with the property manager and asks about her day. "I know I'm way down on the waitlist, but if a three-bedroom frees up I can take it at any time." The manager likes Ross. He's polite and treats her with more respect than any of her tenants. "Well," she says, "funny you should mention it. We had a contract fall through yesterday afternoon. Let's go check it out. If you're not picky about the location, I can get you in next week."

*Ian*

Ian's plane to Boston has mechanical issues. As he waits to be rerouted, Ian watches people get upset, make urgent phone calls, and lose their tempers. When he approaches the gate attendant, she has a scowl.

Ian says, "Honestly, I don't travel often. I'm sorry, but I really don't know what to do next to make it to my meeting tomorrow. Can you please help me?" The gate agent's face softens and she replies, "It looks like you haven't checked a bag. Here's a ticket. If you can get to Gate E16 in the next thirty minutes, we can get you on that plane. You'll have to hurry, but there shouldn't be any trouble." Ian thanks her. She replies, "Thank *you*. Have a good meeting and please fly us again sometime soon."

Ian doesn't know it, but the attendant chooses to treat him better than some of the more seasoned travelers with status because he was courteous and kind. Like many service providers, she has the authority and discretion to improve her customer's situation.

When you make requests, do it with courtesy. Treat everyone at every level with respect. Why would you talk down to the person who can help you the most? Receptionists, waitstaff, dry cleaners, and taxi drivers deserve as much respect as business owners and high-level executives. These hardworking people make the difference between a great experience and a bad one. You might be surprised at who they know and how much power they wield.

### Stefan

Stefan watches how Bob, his colleague, talks to the server at the restaurant and is embarrassed. The server has gone out of his way to make sure they have a nice evening. Bob is supposed to be some super salesperson. He's not being very super right now.

### Ask to Listen

Asking gives you an opportunity to connect and to LISTEN! Everyone wants to be heard. People who feel heard form better relationships with you and communicate more freely. Stop formulating your response before listening to their responses. Ask questions, explore their answers, and listen for what is said and what isn't.

Good listening begins with the method of communication people prefer. You are more likely to have stronger connections and more meaningful conversations.

### Communication mode

The general rule is to *respond* to another person's message in the same manner the message was sent. Check your assumptions, though. Ask about preferences in communicating.

- "How would you like to communicate: by email, text, or phone, or in person?"
- "Before we begin, what's the best way to connect?"
- "Is there anything to avoid when I'm trying to reach you?"
- "Whom should I reach out to if you and I have trouble connecting?"

To improve response times and sharing of information, know and honor how someone wants to receive your messages and requests. Even if you think they *should* communicate the way you wish, figure out what works. Communicate in a way that prompts the other person to respond.

### Ryan

Ryan is fed up with his disrespectful teammates. When he emails them, no one responds. He tells his coworker, who replies, "Text them. They always respond to texts." Doubtful, Ryan texts his teammates, and reminds them to join the phone conference in five minutes. Five minutes later, his teammates log on to the conference call line. Ryan determines that sending one group text is better than sending several unanswered emails and attending the conference calls alone.

If you feel you are missing out on information, check to see if there is a communication or technical glitch. See if there is a good reason you were excluded. There may be a misunderstanding or an issue unrelated to you.

### Brynn

Brynn has not been responding to Laura's text messages. No matter what Laura sends, Brynn is silent. Laura racks her brain to figure out what she did to upset Brynn. When the two finally talk, Laura asks, "What's up? Why aren't you answering my texts?" Brynn says she didn't receive any texts from Laura and looks at her phone. Brynn discovers that for the last two days her phone had been placed on a setting that blocked Laura's texts and several others.

If you find you aren't receiving emails, calendar invites, or are left off emails, go to the source and/or ask another person to copy you. Often they weren't being disrespectful; you were added after the chain began. Also, ask people not to copy you on every email but only the ones that need your attention. And avoid responding to all on your own emails.

*I asked my team members to only send me emails that need my attention. Instead of reading 500 extraneous emails, my request saved me a few hours a day. This allowed me to focus on leading my team members. Now they feel more connected as well.*

### Live in the question

Questions help you seek clarification, understand the unexpected, know when to take action, and know what to avoid. The best questions help you gain information and allow others to reflect on their true objectives.

Mina Brown, coauthor of *Quick Start Coaching Kit: The Fast Track to Coaching Success,* says that to really know a person, you need to "ask open-ended questions and listen with 'big ears.' Listen for what is said and what is not." Remind yourself to be present as people discuss their answers or describe their reasoning. Repeat exactly what you hear and ask if that is what they said.

### "What" and "how"

To have the most meaningful conversations, use the executive coaches' technique of asking "what" and "how" questions. These words bring forth a wealth of information because they are nonjudgmental. The questions are respectful and allow the listener to remain curious instead of providing solutions.

Open-ended questions seek answers that require more than a yes or no. Because they are nonjudgmental, they promote discussion instead of causing listeners to guard against attack. Usually, you can receive the same information you are seeking without a defensive answer.

> "How are you going to ensure you're on time tomorrow?"
> "What was the reason for driving so fast?"
> "How can you rewrite this paper to make it better"

### Why not "why"?

If possible, avoid asking questions that begin with "why." That word focuses on the problem instead of the solution. Often, when people hear "why," they rationalize and defend themselves. And avoiding "why" questions also avoids the dreaded response "Because I said so!"

### Your opinion

Resist the urge to give your opinion when people ask you to help them think through a problem. Go to questions to seek clarity first.

> "What have you thought about?"
> "What questions are you asking yourself?"
> "What would be helpful to hear?"
> "How will that decision impact you?"

People know what is best for them deep down. Often, they just need to think through options or receive validation. Try these questions to help them determine their next step or take action.

"It sounds like you are on the right track. What are you going to do?"

"Considering those options, what direction are you leaning?"

"If you couldn't fail, what would you try?"

"If you were advising your best friend who was experiencing the same situation, what would you suggest to him or her?"

Additional coaching questions can be found at AskOutrageously.com.

---

### Action Asks

Instead of providing the advice or recommendation, ask what should be done. Usually people know their best next step and are more committed to taking action:

- "Now that you've shared this concern, how would you like to proceed?"
- "With everything we've discussed, what's our next step?"
- "How do you best want to address this?"
- "What do you want to do next? How committed are you to taking that action?"

---

You don't have to provide your opinion and offer advice in response to every question people ask, even if you have a really great answer. Each situation is unique. People usually have the wisdom they need, and they are more likely to take action on a solution they themselves create.

### Watch body language

In addition to listening to others, watch their body language. Asking allows you an opportunity to watch behavior. If you see someone make an abrupt change with a gesture, in body positioning, or with a facial expression, pay attention. You may be picking up a signal about how your message is landing.

Be careful assuming you can read people's intentions. You can't know exactly what is taking place in their brains or the reason their bodies are reacting. For example, if you speak of something they disagree with, they may wrinkle their noses in disgust or touch it to show disbelief. Perhaps they squint their eyes to understand better or blink more frequently because they are lying. Maybe they touch their chins as they deeply consider your request. And, of course, maybe all of these reactions are related to allergies or a cold. Leaning forward may indicate an interest in your conversation and leaning back could show they are soaking in your words. And the same gestures could mean their backs are tired and that they want to change posture or position. Crossing their arms may signal they are closed or finished with the discussion. However, many would tell you that they're more relaxed sitting that way.

When you see someone's body language change, ask:

"How is that landing with you?"

"Do you agree with that point?"

"What are you thinking about now?"

"I notice you don't look as enthusiastic about that question. Can you share your thoughts?"

Remember that different gestures carry very different meanings depending on the culture. Nodding, eye contact, touching someone when talking, personal space, and time sensitivity can convey very different messages depending on where you are.

---

**Pay attention to your body language. Are the signals your behavior sends congruent with the message you want communicated?**

---

### Silence

Ask and then give others time to answer. People need time to think and for ideas to simmer. Don't fill that silence with nervous chatter. And don't withdraw your request before you have an answer. You may have been thinking of this request awhile, but it is brand new to them. Give others the ability to think of a response worthy of your request. Waiting in silence can take a tremendous amount of willpower. Here are some ways to keep your mouth shut and your options open:

- Count to ten or beyond.
- Remind yourself that it's respectful to allow someone else to think.
- On the phone, press mute. (Take yourself off mute when it's your turn to speak.)
- While on the phone, bite your knuckle or tongue, literally.
- Observe your breathing. Focus on relaxing and staying calm.
- Observe the other person and his or her body language.
- Remember that you probably aren't waiting as long as you think.

---

**Learn to be comfortable with silence.**

---

### Respect what people tell you

People feel respected when you listen and give them what they want. In return, they provide you more information and are more likely to be your advocates later.

#### Trey

A technology sales representative for the trucking industry, Trey attended a discovery meeting to find out what software was needed for delivery vehicles. Trey asked, "Why are we here today? What problem do you want to solve?" The potential client was clear. "We only want the software to do two things: keep us legal and make sure our drivers always know where they are going."

One competitor did a total operational review and showed efficiencies the prospect was losing throughout its entire operation. Trey chose a different approach. "We didn't have the most advanced software, and we weren't the least expensive. However, I heard my prospect say what they wanted," Trey explains. "Instead of a complete demo on the nine applications our software offered, I took a risk and focused my entire pitch around the two solutions they wanted." Listening to his customer paid off. "I won the business over seven competitors and their teams." That one sale met three months of quota and firmly placed Trey as the top salesperson in both units and revenue.

## True or False: Don't Speak First

Have you been told if you speak first after asking a question, you lose your advantage? The theory is that speaking too soon communicates that you have a weaker position and are uneasy or even desperate.

Speaking too quickly can show excitement or interrupt the other person's thought process. Realistically, though, what are you going to do if both of you have heard that advice? Sit in silence and stare at each other? Instead, ask questions one at a time and allow people to think. If the person looks confused or didn't hear you, repeat or rephrase your question and wait for his or her response.

If you want respect, respect others. Listen. Genuinely consider their opinions or concerns. Acknowledge their experiences and perceptions. Help people feel at ease.

*Nelly*

When Raymond, a new medical assistant, meets with department head Nelly, he notices her office decor. Flowered curtains match the chair cushions. Around the office, he sees plants and inspirational pictures. When he asks Nelly why her office is different from everyone else's, she responds, "People who see us are in a stressful situation. They are here to learn the treatment options to battle an intimidating diagnosis. We want our patients to feel comfortable so they can ask any questions they need answered."

### Rules of respect and engagement

When you face a meeting in which topics can get heated, you'll find that courtesy, respect, and trust occur more frequently when you ask for a commitment up front.

Learn from experts who facilitate, mediate, and moderate difficult discussions. They know the secret to managing meetings, especially when participants attempt to dominate conversations or face conflict.

These experts ask participants to define desired outcomes and behaviors *before* entering into discussions. Agreed-upon rules of engagement can include asking: Is honoring time important? Are you silencing phones? Are the topics confidential? Can we agree to open and candid conversation?

Author of *On My Honor, I Will*, Randy Pennington says that the parties in union negotiation talks assume everyone is looking out for his or her own best interests. He asks people,

"What do we need to know and feel about how information is shared to make this a successful negotiation?"

Once people agree to basic rules of conduct, they are more likely to honor their promises and monitor their behavior. Agreement to strong rules of engagement creates a safe environment that allows for candid conversation and even heated debates.

### Three Leaders

Three community action group leaders are meeting with a facilitator. Instead of communicating and collaborating, they argue and compete for attention and resources. After the leaders rehash past deeds and point fingers, the facilitator makes a request of each leader: "Pretend you belong to a different group. Now use the same passion you feel for your group to make a request on behalf of your new group." The result is phenomenal. Once the leaders' defenses are down, they discover new opportunities to assist each other. Together, they make larger requests, support each other's efforts, and improve the likelihood of achieving their outcomes.

Jeff Blackman, author of *Stop Whining! Start Selling!*, has a technique he uses to check if his audience understands his point. Instead of saying "Did you understand?" or "Did everyone get that?" he places the obligation to clearly communicate on himself. His question is "How well have I explained that?"

The *wording* of requests matters. Research shows that not enough attention is placed on using words that can improve relationships and build trust with the people who can grant the request. What can you say to show you mean them no harm and are fair? How do you help them let down their guard to listen to your request or grant an exception?

### Ask to get out of a traffic ticket

A frequent request is to get out of a traffic ticket. Of the people surveyed in the Ask Outrageously Study, 33 percent said they had asked to get out of a traffic ticket and were successful (see page 99). If you are among the 67 percent who would never ask or have been unsuccessful, Traci Brown, a body language expert and author of *Persuasion Points: Body Language and Speech for Influence* offers this advice.

"The best way to avoid a traffic ticket is to obey the law," Traci says. "The second best way is to show respect and appreciation for the police officer's authority through your tone of voice, your manner, and by keeping your hands on the wheel." She advises to wait until you are asked to get your documents and then say, "My license is in my purse and my insurance is in my glove box. Is it OK if I get them?"

Courteous, respectful, and non-threatening requests work the best with law officers and with everyone else.

### Good intentions

Don't assume someone has confidence in you or your motives. Ask if the person has reservations or is committed. If you can determine his or her potential concerns, you are much closer to addressing issues and connecting powerfully. To find out if your request seems fair and is in the other person's best interests, simply ask.

> "Now that we've discussed our action steps, what questions do you have?"

> "With all that we've discussed, does this seem like a reasonable request?"

Finding out about issues of trust early is preferred. Although *you* know you have good intentions, *they* may not know you are trustworthy. They may have had experiences with others who weren't honest or didn't treat them fairly.

## Play Fair

You don't want to cheat others. However, the opportunity to take advantage can be real: you could benefit because of an imbalance of power, or maybe you know information they don't. You don't want to hurt people or ruin their businesses.

### Sylvia

Sylvia is charged with finding at least a 5 percent cost savings on all expenditures with suppliers. Expecting to encounter some pushback, she asks for a savings of 10 percent across the board. Two of her suppliers give the 10 percent discount to her without question, four offer 5 percent, and one flat-out refuses.

Sylvia wants to be fair. She doesn't want to take advantage of the two who offered the full discount. They always do her favors and provide excellent services. Sylvia decides the most equitable decision is to require the same discount from all. She contacts each supplier and tells them she needs a 7 percent discount from each. Her response shows her favorite suppliers she isn't greedy, and 7 percent isn't a big jump for those who offered 5 percent. The supplier who offered her no discount is given an opportunity to meet the 7 percent or no longer do business with the company. Sylvia looks great to her boss and, with the extra 2 percent, shouldn't have to ask for a reduction for a while.

Would people do the work if you weren't around to monitor it? Do they trust the information you provide or seek confirmation first? What would most people say if you made a mistake on an agreement? They could say "no worries" or "too bad—we agreed." How sure are you of the responses you would get?

### Jessie

Jessie sends her signed portion of the staffing agreement to the client. A few moments later, she realizes she sent the wrong contract. The language could hurt her company if the client enforces the contract. She calls up her client and says, "I'm sorry. I didn't review what I sent you carefully enough. It's our old agreement and it has the wrong language." Jessie holds her breath and waits for the response. Her client says, "It's not a problem. We wondered. That agreement didn't look like what we agreed. We are shredding it now. Send us the correct one and we'll get it signed."

## People are watching

Pay attention, especially if you are in a position of influencing or leading others. People notice your actions as well as your lack of action. They witness your demeanor to others. They observe how kind, generous, and trustworthy you act. They consider your behavior when you ask them to do something. Think about these examples of respect erosion:

### Fred and Ted

Fred and Ted are supervisors in a plastics manufacturing plant. They are sticklers for enforcing tardiness, breaks, and lunch times. However, every morning at 10:15 they stretch *their* fifteen-minute smoke break to twenty-five minutes or more.

### *Jenna*

Jenna looks at the billing report. It isn't accurate. She spent days at two clients' offices. However, Jenna's senior partner reduced her reported hours and inflated his time at his higher billing rate. Not only are the partner's actions unethical, they are also detrimental. The client will pay a significantly higher bill, and Jenna will lose internal credit for her hours because they aren't billed.

### *Your fair share*

At work do you do your fair share? Are you considered a team player? If not, practice helping out with something that is not your job or responsibility. For example, answer the phone for a busy coworker, offer to make copies, open doors, handle a project for a co-worker who is swamped, or mentor someone. Ask to serve others in a way you usually wouldn't.

### *Who can you trust?*

Sometimes others are given more trust because of the roles or positions they hold. Religious leaders, doctors, lawyers, police officers, counselors, teachers, day care providers, senior care medical personnel, nurses, financial professionals, public servants, firefighters, members of the military, and food providers often receive trust. They can be given great power and trusted to do the right thing with money, safety, lives, and loved ones. They control what you don't know or can't check. Due to this power, they are held to high standards and are required to comply with professional ethical codes and standards.

When these trusted advisors violate the trust they are granted or are involved in unethical behaviors, there is a fear the world is not as dependable or safe as we had thought or hoped. Consider the media headlines when someone overreaches, abuses, or violates the interests of others or the respected position they hold. Dave Lieber, an author, reporter, and nationally syndicated columnist, suggests doing quick background checks on service providers to make sure you aren't burned. Dave says, "Don't wait for [others] to protect you. It's best to know a company's tricks, be on guard, and stay suspicious…. We must question them, test them, and coldly reject them when we get a warning sign, through our watchdog instincts, that all is not right."

Treat everyone with respect and act honorably—even when you think no one is watching you. When faced with a situation in which your ethics might be compromised, ask yourself how media headlines about you would read or what a jury member might think of your actions. Also, how would you explain your request or decision to someone you respect? If people can't trust you, they won't respect you.

### Ways to rebuild trust and respect

When you make a mistake or breach a confidence, you need to rebuild trust. Eric Harvey, president of the Walk the Talk Company, explains that you have to ask for forgiveness *before* you can ask for trust.

> First you need to admit the importance of trust to any personal or professional relationship. Tell the other party, "I realize you have lost trust with me. I want to gain it back." Then ask, "Will you let me attempt to rebuild your trust?" Thank that person for that opportunity. Be sure to check in with the person in the future to assure your trust has been reestablished.

Companies also have to rebuild trust with their customers when mistakes occur. They need to acknowledge the mistake, ask for forgiveness, and state what they are going to do to solve the issues. In this digital age, keeping that trust may involve getting a message out in real time and updating with developments as you learn them.

### Lead Others to Ask

Here are some activities to help you create higher levels of trust and respect among the people you lead or coach:

- Engage meeting attendees by delegating meeting functions such as time keeping and reporting.
- Discourage multi-tasking by virtual attendees by keeping track of participation and directing questions to those who don't speak.
- Create scenarios related to trust and respect. Have your people practice the questions to ask when they find themselves in potentially compromising situations.
- Review your compensation plans, internal contents, policies, and procedures to make sure that employees aren't encouraged to game the system to improve rankings, numbers, or compensation.
- Ask your direct reports to create their own rules-of-engagement meetings. Ask others to help enforce these rules during meetings.

For a list of powerful rules of engagement that work in meeting management, go to AskOutrageously.com.

### Outrageous Review

- Asking gives you an opportunity to listen. When you listen, you show respect, build trust, and gain more information.
- Knowing how someone prefers to receive information—text, email, phone, in person—will increase your chances of getting a yes.

- When you are privy to information unknown to the other party, then you have the opportunity to take advantage of that person. Taking advantage does not build trust.
- Ask "what" and "how" questions because answers to these questions focus on the solution and the future.
- Avoid asking "why" questions when making requests. "Why" questions can make others defensive.
- Handle an advantage diplomatically.
- Treat everyone at every level with respect—even when you think no one is watching you. People are more likely to deny a request if the person asking is inconsiderate or has bad manners.

## Smart Asks

- Do I know someone's preferred means of communication? Ask, "Would you prefer me to call or email you?"
- What can I do to help others trust and respect me more?
- Where am I cutting corners in my life or job that could lead me to make unethical decisions?
- What excuses do I make that can cause others not to trust me? (Rationalizations for not doing what is right include "Everyone does it," "No one will ever know or care," and "That's close enough.")
- Am I behaving in a way that aligns with my integrity or am I just trying to please others?

## Ask List

- Keep information given to you confidential, even if it is great gossip.
- Listen without interrupting someone.
- Drive the speed limit everywhere you go this week.
- Arrive early for an appointment or meeting.

- No matter how you are treated or how stressed you feel at the moment, *please* remember to be polite, courteous, and respectful with your requests. *Thank you.*

### Secret Success Tools

For a list of powerful "Rules of Engagement" that work in meeting management and building trust, go to AskOutrageously. com.

# Six

# Ask Everywhere– All the Time

You have heard the advice that "practice makes perfect" or "*perfect* practice makes perfect." The belief is that you should practice the correct way, every time, in order to improve. However, when it comes to asking, perfect practice *prevents* better results. Here's why. *You* aren't perfect. You will never be perfect, never ask perfectly, and never get a perfect result. Focusing on *perfecting* the way you make requests keeps you from asking and practicing. When it comes to asking outrageously, practice all the time to prove to yourself that making requests leads to positive results.

What happens if you aren't bold but want to improve your ability to ask? You practice asking, everywhere, until you *are* bold (see Figure 6). Make requests outside your comfort zone. Go to places no one knows you and just practice asking.

This strategy makes the risk of asking less risky and desensitizes you to the experience. It is a way to experience the process of making outrageous requests with minimal threat. For example, at the grocery store, ask fellow shoppers if they like the brand of bread they are buying. Quiz the people working at the deli counter. Ask if there are specials you should know about. Ask a store employee to go to the back to find an item.

---

### Don't practice to make perfect— practice to provide proof.

---

Don't stop at the grocery store. Test the concept. Go to flea markets, garage sales, yard sales. Make your first attempts on items you don't care if you win. Ask for free samples when they aren't being handed out. Then be brazen in your requests. Shoot for the moon. Know what is reasonable and then ask for something unreasonable. Ask for more or much larger than you deserve at no additional charge. Ask for an outrageous discount or bargain. Offer a lowball price for something you don't need but wouldn't mind having. Offer such a low figure it would never be considered seriously. Stand there. Smile. Be pleasant. Then observe.

### *Jimi*

When Jimi goes to the office supply store to buy three print cartridges, the total rings up $100 more than she thinks they should cost. Before paying, she asks the cashier to check the price on the store's website. As he searches the store site, a line forms behind Jimi. While she waits for confirmation on the cartridge listed price, Jimi makes one more request. "Do you have a coupon I can use?" Surprisingly, the cashier pulls one out of the cash drawer. When Jimi finally leaves the store, she has three cartridges priced correctly, a discount from the coupon, and a *bonus package* of free photo paper that came with the print cartridges. Score!

Small asks become bigger asks, which become outrageous asks. Watch as you grow and graduate to bolder asks. Next, you'll

**Figure 6**
**Professionally, have you ever asked for ...**

Better terms from a supplier or vendor?

More time to complete a project?

A client referral?

An introduction for a job interview?

A change in work group/team or department?

A raise or promotion?

Better office space?

More vacation time or personal time?

An apology from a coworker or boss?

A change in bosses?

- Would never ask
- No, but wouldn't mind asking
- Yes, but was not successful
- Yes, and got what I wanted
- Yes, and got more than I wanted

0    200   400   600   800  1000  1200

begin to fearlessly request finance options. Then you will ask for the waiver of fees when buying a home. Soon you will be asking for your own office—or even your own office building.

## Talk to Strangers

Forget what your parents told you about strangers being scary and unsafe. Practice with people you don't know. They are perfect. You will never see them again. They have no preconceived ideas about you. As long as you are in a public place and they look relatively safe, they are fair game to participate in your self-development. Most people are willing to give advice or opinions. So ask them.

---

**Hold a garage sale to witness people's asking behavior. Notice how many people make outrageous requests. Watch these masters of asking in their element.**

---

Practice with hotel front desk clerks, restaurant waitstaff, and service providers. Ask for a better table, a better room, a free dessert, or an upgraded service at no additional charge. Help them serve you even better by practicing your respectful requests with them. Ignore what you've been taught about being greedy or asking for seconds. You won't surprise the seasoned professionals. They hear requests all the time. Watch how they grant or turn down a request while maintaining a relationship with the customer.

### Interrupt someone

Interrupt someone who should be serving you. Walk up to an employee who is talking about weekend plans to a coworker, texting, or pretending to be busy. Patiently wait until they observe you and then politely ask for help.

"Excuse me, I hate to interrupt you but ..."

"I'm sorry to interrupt your work ..."

Think about it. You don't mind being interrupted as long as people are considerate. You are worthy of politely interrupting someone to make a request. And, of course, they wouldn't have a job without customers like you.

## Be a polite disruptor.

At this point, you may be saying, "Really. You want me to bother strangers or interrupt a person who is hard at work?" Yes. Resist the temptation to walk away. No matter whom you interrupt for help, pay close attention to the person's reactions—and to your own.

Discover how *you* feel when someone acts as if you are keeping them from the very "important" task of grocery shopping or stocking items on a shelf. Politely disturb employees talking about their latest romantic encounter, a fantasy football team, or which tattoo would look better. *Interrupt and ask a question.* Wow! What nerve you have. How can you *bother* a salesperson who is paid to help you?

Some people may look flustered or perturbed, or roll their eyes. You'll get a few of those responses. Process these reactions as feedback only. If they have an issue with doing their jobs, it's *their* issue. You can decide then if you have crossed a line and should apologize, or if you should make another request.

In all practice requests, become a neutral observer. Do your best to manage your emotions. Identify which requests are easiest to make and when asking isn't worth your time or energy. When do you feel uneasy or just want to leave? Watch to discover which approaches work and which don't.

Practice on your family. They are the toughest. Ask them for something outrageous like performing extra chores or going with you to a movie instead of seeing their friends. If you can persuade your own family, you can persuade practically anyone.

### Ask at Work

In their professional lives, survey respondents reported that they feel most comfortable asking for a client referral, more time to complete a project, or better terms from a vendor (see Figure 6).

For some people, asking at work is easier than asking in their personal lives. Ask for the work you like that uses your talents. If you are a good employee, it is in your boss's best interests to keep you happy, productive, and doing work for which you are best suited.

---

### What Can You Ask For at Work?

- Ask a long-term vendor for free shipping or a discount.
- Ask if someone new wants to go to lunch.
- Ask for help from a colleague.
- Ask for an opinion on a project.
- Ask if you can attend a meeting with your boss.
- Ask a peer to be a subject matter expert on your next team call or in a meeting.
- Ask a friend to critique your presentation.
- Ask for an internship.
- Ask to partner on a project.
- Ask to get experience in other departments or receive specialized training.
- Ask for opportunities to lead a team or a special initiative.

---

### *Gina*

Gina sees that one of the departments at her company is pioneering a new process for clean water in developing countries. Although it is outside her scope, she approaches the team leader and asks how she can be a part of the project.

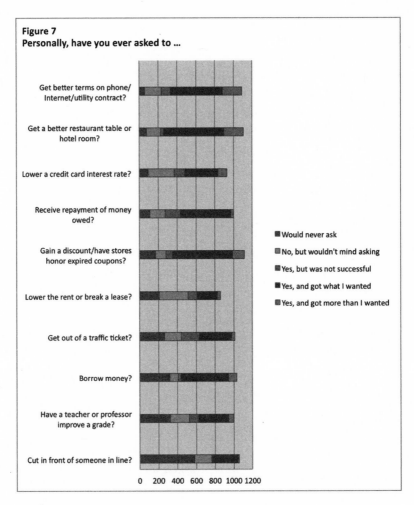

**Figure 7**
**Personally, have you ever asked to …**

*Antonio*

Antonio tells his boss he likes making presentations and training others. He asks her if there are more opportunities to do this type of work. Once his boss knows of his interest, she gives him speaking roles in meetings and shifts speaking responsibilities from two coworkers who don't like that aspect of their jobs. She also volunteers Antonio to do training in other departments.

### Frank

After seeing a documentary on the possibilities of using renewable resources, Frank has an interest in encouraging a green effort in his manufacturing company. He does further research on the Internet and joins some online communities. Frank brings the idea to a leader in his company's design and development team. The leader agrees to sponsor a pilot project on three products to determine if there is a market for green alternatives.

### Concentrated asking

Pursuant to their seminar, three high-potential leaders in construction agree to practice asking outrageously professionally and personally for one week. Although they were outside their comfort zone, these rising leaders didn't ask for the impossible. As they began focusing on *what* they wanted and asked for it, their requests grew bigger and more frequent. When you concentrate on what you're seeking and ask, breakthroughs occur everywhere and all the time.

### Mandy

Mandy asked professionally and personally. At the end of the week she reported, "First, I asked a customer to send me a large change order he had been holding back so I could bill it this month. He did. Then I asked my dog's vet to waive his office visit fee as I have been a good and loyal paying customer. He did. Last, I asked my subcontractor to drop his pricing on a change order to help me help a customer. Done!"

### Shannon

Shannon reported a few asks of her own that week. Here is what she said about her three successful asks. "Currently we are pushing technology to our field leadership but we are still using paper forms. To eliminate paperwork, I asked if we could create electronic forms. *Yes!* The leader on one of my projects suggested a reasonable timeline of one year. I asked if we could do it in six months. The leader agreed! My fiancé agreed to purchase a wedding band—if I found one within our budget."

### Brian

Brian had similar results. "First, I asked my client for a two-week extension on the project, which I thought he would deny. To my surprise, he accepted one week! Also, I have been dealing with a back charge of $20,000 to one of my subcontractors for months via email. I decided to meet in person with the owner and discuss the situation. After meeting and explaining the issue, he accepted!" Brian had a personal request, too. "I asked my wife if she is ready for kid number three. To my surprise she said yes."

What would be possible if you worked together with others to support each other? When a team is motivated, they come up with innovative ideas that save time and money. They also decrease your headaches. Here are some results when individual team members began asking for improvements at the same time.

*We improved delivery times, in some cases by a week (a 50 percent improvement), by asking.*

*One of the ideas we asked for and implemented saved us $90,000 annually.*

*We asked our manufacturers to provide the equipment, safety gear, and some instruction materials at no cost to use in our training facility. Now our trainees can experience the real equipment and procedures they will need.*

*We successfully requested $5,000 off an entertainment package we put together for next year's conference.*

### Ask for more business

In the research, the most popular professional request is asking for more business from current clients. Sixty-six percent reported they have asked for a client referral and got one or more (see page 95).

Contact your current clients and ask them for more business! Here are some examples of how to word your request:

"I really like working with you. What other projects do you think we could work on together?"

---

**Bragging for Business**

How do you market and tell others how great you are when you are raised not to brag? Try these ideas:

- Be truthful about your background and the solutions you provide.
- Write case studies revealing actual problems and how your company fixed them.
- Ask for testimonials from happy clients and their permission to use them in your marketing materials and online.
- Share what distinguishes your business offerings from other businesses (for example, timing, quality, pricing, customer attention). Your potential clients want to know the differences so they can choose their best solution.

"With the outcomes we just reviewed, what opportunities do you see for the upcoming year?"

You can also ask clients for referrals to new clients:

"You and your business are a perfect fit for my company. Do you know of other people like you who might need my services?"

"I noticed you are connected with someone I've always wanted to do business with. Would you send an email connecting me with your contact at XYZ Company and tell them what you think about the services I provide?"

No matter how well you're liked, people may forget about helping you unless you ask. You aren't bragging or boasting. Instead you are letting people know about the services and products you provide. You are asking others to make appropriate introductions to people you could serve well.

*I asked outrageously and reconnected with two clients I haven't heard much from in the last year. We have successfully begun dialogue, discussing possible options later this year where they may need support.*

### Tamara

Business coach Tamara Hamilton wanted more speaking engagements. She asks other coaches in her District of Columbia and Virginia network for help getting presentation work. By asking about work in a few of her social media groups, she was asked to do a seminar at the White House and in several federal agencies.

By asking people who like working with you for more business and for referrals, you reveal to them that you can handle more clients or other types of work. Done professionally and consistently, the practice of asking for more work allows you to keep your calendar full and stay top of mind for future business.

---

*When in doubt, always go to a question.*
                                    **— Attorney-Mediators Institute**

---

### Benefits to speaking up

Staying silent after you ask is powerful. However, keeping quiet when you should speak up is demotivating. For example, when a client asks you to reduce your reasonable service fee for no legitimate reason, you can ask yourself where you prefer to donate your time. "Do I really want to give my time and services to someone who received value and has the funds to pay me? Or do I prefer to donate my time to a non-profit I'm passionate about that can't afford my fees?" Staying silent can result in loss of income and be the source of regrets that you didn't ask.

### Ask during job interviews

Stay focused on what you want during the stressful interview process. Study respondents reported that they wished they had paid better attention and requested more compensation, moving expenses, more vacation time, or better benefits before they were hired. They regretted not exploring the options or preparing themselves better to make requests during the interview process. Ginger Shelhimer, head of Mergers and Acquisitions HR at Ericsson, has some pointed advice:

> Be prepared when negotiating salary. Prior to asking, do the research to establish the current market value of your skills. Then ask for what you are worth in a way that allows both you

and the potential employer to win. You get the job and your employer gets the talent they need.

Once you are hired at a particular salary, you will be frustrated if you discover that people newer to the company are making more money or receive benefits you could have had if you had asked.

*When doing performance reviews for my direct reports, I found out they were making more than I was. They didn't have my expertise, experience, or responsibilities. My boss adjusted my compensation when I showed him the documentation. However, it wouldn't have happened if I hadn't spotted the disparity and asked.*

### Raises and Promotions

Asking for money is intimidating, especially when it's for a raise. In the Ask Outrageously Study, 10 percent of people said they would never ask for a raise (see page 95). There are even people who prefer to look for another job rather than ask for a raise or promotion in their current job.

*Asking for a raise sounds like you are threatening your boss. It implies you are going to leave if you don't get one. It sounds like you are making an ultimatum.*

*If the company is getting ready to do layoffs, you could jeopardize your job.*

*It's a risky move. Your boss may not have received a raise lately either.*

*Most bosses don't have authority to give you a raise.*

*If it's not the right time in the corporate cycle, asking for a raise is fruitless.*

Good news! The odds are in your favor. More people who asked for a raise were successful than failed. Take a look at these statistics from the Ask Outrageously Study:

■ 17 percent of respondents asked for a raise and did not get what they wanted.

■ 42 percent of respondents asked for a raise and got what they asked for, with another 9 percent getting *more* than they asked for.

According to the study, the top three things people will do before asking for a raise (ranked in order of popularity) are:

1. Find out what they need to do to be considered and take action.
2. Go online or research what others are paid in their job and profession.
3. Seek advice from someone in leadership they know.

Websites such as Glassdoor.com, Monster.com, and Recruiter. com provide advice about companies, culture, and job salaries. Whether you are seeking employment, hoping to get a promotion, or want to hire a professional, check out the online posts and ratings. You may be pleasantly surprised or shocked by what people say about your organization.

### Be prepared if you hear yes

Your boss may not know you are interested or may be unaware of a situation. In any case, ask big in case your supervisor agrees.

*That afternoon, I went to see my boss and asked for the raise I was promised. He gave it to me. He honestly didn't know I hadn't received it yet.*

*I asked if I could apply for the job. My supervisor said I hadn't worked there long enough and didn't have the exact experience for the role but agreed to make an exception. Although I had been there only nine months and didn't have a four-year degree, I got the promotion and several more after that.*

Your request may lead your supervisor to ask leadership on your behalf. By giving your supervisors a business justification and evidence of your abilities, you'll help them when they make the request to their bosses.

### Be prepared to hear no

Just like other people, managers sometimes need to let a new idea, such as a raise, percolate. You may have been thinking about asking for several months, but your request is new information to them. Occasionally, you'll encounter a boss who offers but won't or can't deliver. By asking, you'll find out where you stand. In a bad situation, you can apply for a transfer or look for another opportunity.

*My boss says yes but means no. She'll say … Sure you can have a raise, but you first need to jump through these fifty hoops with documentation supporting your preparation, your prediction, and the outcomes … If I like all of your answers … I might think of talking to my boss … but then again, I may make you ask me and do this exercise five more times before you get tired of it all and simply move on.*

### Know your strategy if you are turned down

For instance, say, "I appreciate your point of view/understand the financial state of the company right now. What do I need to do to earn consideration for a raise or promotion in the future?" Then work on any areas identified and show your progress.

*Dietrich*

Dietrich wants to understand his development areas to enhance his ability to advance. His supervisor doesn't want to dampen Dietrich's enthusiasm or paint an unrealistic picture of future promotions. Dietrich asks, "I know there are no positions available right now, but I want to be ready. When you compare my performance with the performance of people you've managed and promoted, what two or three development areas would you recommend I improve in?"

### Assess what you are bringing to the organization

Showing up and doing your job is expected. Make sure you are seen as a positive presence, someone who pitches in and is an asset to coworkers. Evaluate how you add to the organization's bottom line, improve processes, or reduce costs. Before you ask for a raise or promotion, make a realistic list of your accomplishments and value to the organization. Dare to include the valuable things you have done.

> *My position was just promoted, but HR did not want to use the title I proposed. I decided to ask again. This time I explained my reasoning. My request worked. The financial gain to me is zero, but the emotional gain is great.*

Keep a "love me" file with letters and emails from people who said you made a difference. Review your accomplishments when preparing to approach your boss for a raise or promotion or when you need a little motivation. Prove to yourself first that you add value, and you'll feel more confident when you make your request. Ask yourself, "What would I say to someone who has done what I have?" Admit it. You have a good reputation. You deliver on your promises. Even if you aren't granted a request, the groundwork you lay today may have unintended effects.

### Marguerite

At a national sales meeting, Marguerite boldly asked a senior executive to come out to her territory to talk with a customer. Marguerite says, "My customer was the head of purchasing for one of my hospital systems. The system was nowhere near large enough to be named a national account; but still, it was important to the business in my geography. They were using my less expensive product and would not move to my more expensive one." The senior executive made an appearance. The customer was impressed that such a senior-level person would come to visit the hospital. "We still didn't get them to switch, BUT I had valuable time impressing the brass by proving my product knowledge and selling savvy. When it came time for my review, my numbers fell short on selling the more expensive product. However, I felt comfortable that I had done what I could, AND I knew that business wasn't being moved to my competition. I'm so glad I asked!"

## Look forward

You have already been paid for the work you did in the past. Rehashing your previous accomplishments should not be your goal. Instead, focus on solutions you can bring during the upcoming year. Use your past as proof you will achieve future results. Help your boss "sell" or justify increasing your pay to his or her boss, human resources, or other leaders.

### Jamie

Makeup artist Jamie spent weeks thinking about how the store could sell more make-up to a younger clientele. She wants to build on her success from the past year. Instead of discussing her ideas, the store owner puts Jamie's writtten plan in a drawer to "consider later." Jamie feels dismissed, as if her ideas aren't taken seriously. Before leaving, Jamie asks for clarification.

"I saw you put my plans in the drawer. What's up?" The owner: "Jamie, we are having corporate tax issues. I can't give your ideas my full attention until Friday." Jamie realizes the postponement has nothing to do with her. She says, "Thanks for clearing that up. Want to talk next Tuesday?"

### Ask to get ahead

Be prepared, take a deep breath, and *ask*. Do not stop yourself because you think you might be turned down or you don't have the perfect words. Your boss may think you're content with the money you're making or the role you have. Your job is to let them know you want more compensation or an opportunity to advance, and you are willing to work for the increase in money or responsibility.

Sometimes you already perform the job functions but are not compensated or formally recognized as holding that position.

*My coworkers pointed to me when asked who fit the description of someone who leads without a title. I hadn't seen myself as a leader until I heard one described. I asked for the open leadership position and have been promoted twice since then. I went from twenty years as a front-line worker to manager of a department in six months.*

You are responsible for your own career. No one else has the vested interest in your work, family, and finances that you do ... no one. If great work performance hasn't advanced you to the level you want in your career, it's time to focus on what you really want. Ask for a raise or a promotion. ASK!

### Ask for raise

- Be prepared to hear yes.
- Be prepared to hear no.
- Know your strategy if you are turned down.
- Assess what you bring to the organization.
- Look forward. Help your boss see the future value you'll add.
- ASK. Be prepared. Don't wait for the perfect words or time.

No one is telling you to put your job on the line, gamble your life savings, or take a chance that endangers your life. Start by taking safe risks in safe places. Luck does play a part in the requests you make. And you'll find you get "luckier" the more you ask outrageously. As in Vegas, you have to play if you want the pay. Ask everywhere. Ask all the time.

 **Lead Others to Ask**

Ask people you lead or coach to concentrate on asking outrageously for one week and then report their results. Put your direct reports or teams into accountability groups of three. Make it a contest. See who can get the most for the least or be the most creative. Require them to measure their results in hours, dollars, and/or percentages.

Ask them to tell you how they add value to the company. Have them list their major functions and activities by priority and show ways their efforts could be more valuable.

### Outrageous Review

- Begin paying closer attention to the answers you receive.
- Practice communicating your objectives so someone else can understand your reasoning. Practice asking thoughtful questions about others' needs.

- Practice asking for more and discovering you can live through the experience.
- Get comfortable with the word "no." If you are not hearing no, you are probably not asking for enough. Keep asking until you get the no.
- Create a file of your successes. Use your past results to support requests for future opportunities.

## Smart Asks

- "Who could I ask to help me find an item or assist me?"
- "How could I ask the client I love working with to recommend me to someone in another department?"
- "When I mention I'm working on the new project, my coworker makes a face. I wonder what's up?"
- "How could I show my value to my organization, both now and in the future?"

## Ask List

- Practice being a Polite Disruptor and "Breaking the Rules."
- Ask if you can use an expired coupon or receive a discount.
- Ask to get a free dessert, an upgrade, or a better table.
- Ask a fellow shopper for advice about a purchase or a stranger for information.
- Ask a salesperson for something you want but can't find.

## Secret Success Tool

To download the "List of What You Can Ask For at Work," go to AskOutrageously.com.

# Seven

# Blocks

Before you make a request, it's normal to experience an adrenaline rush, similar to the nervous feeling you get just before you stand up to speak in front of an audience. When you get into a situation that excites you, your brain signals your adrenal glands to produce extra adrenaline. If you're not expecting that surge of power, the energy can throw you off.

The pressure and even anticipation of making a request can change how you process information or communicate. You can plan for the worst, hope for the best, and tell yourself to stay calm. Still, the chemical charge you feel is real. Yet the results of adrenaline are beneficial when you channel them correctly. An adrenaline rush gives you extra energy and makes you more alert. Who doesn't want the advantage of more energy and awareness when you're asking for something big?

## Crushed

Instead of excitement, have you ever felt the anticipation, frustration, or stress was weighing you down, even crushing you? You are concerned and can't figure out your next step. Decisions waiting to be made can pile up on you. You know whatever you request will affect the next decision and the one after that and the ones that follow those. You don't know where to begin. You watch the time tick away. Yet you can't decide how to proceed. You are willing to request help but have no idea whom to ask or what to ask them. Your heart is beating rapidly, your mind is racing, you feel pressure in your chest, your stomach hurts, your head throbs, and nothing makes sense.

Basically, you are supercharged and/or overwhelmed. At the moment, the only *rational* word that comes to mind is "irrational." Nevertheless, psychologist Dr. Mel Whitehurst reminds us, "Fear is a great motivator, perhaps the greatest of all motivators. Mild levels of fear usually coincide with optimal levels of effectiveness."

Quick review: Adrenaline and fear can be beneficial. When in doubt or you don't know what to do, you can always pause a moment to breathe, think, and ask a question. When you can't think of a question to ask, use the ASK Strategy.

### ASK Strategy

When you are in a stressful situation, use the ASK Strategy. This method provides a way to handle most requests and surprising situations, even the most difficult ones.

A: Aware
S: Seek clarification
K: Know your next-best request

You need understanding and calm before you can logically discuss an issue or reach a mutually agreeable outcome. Emotions or reactions can sabotage you and prevent you from thinking clearly and objectively. Instead of allowing emotions to control you, use them as a signal to pay attention and focus on questions to ask next.

## Live in the Moment

Be aware of how stress affects you. Paying attention to your heart rate, your thoughts, your breathing, and how your body feels stress is a start. Once you are aware, you can gain control by becoming more adept at coping strategies.

**A: Aware.** Be aware of what is happening. Start asking yourself questions. What can you determine by someone else's demeanor, words, voice tone, and posture? What about you? What are you aware of right now in this moment in time?

*If you are stressed,* pay attention to how your body is reacting. What are you noticing? For instance, are you breathing too shallowly or quickly? If so, attempt to slow your breath down by counting as you inhale and then as you exhale. Are your eyes tearing up or unable to focus? Be aware of your surroundings. For instance, pay attention to the fabric of your chair, the color of the walls, the flooring.

**S: Seek clarification.** Seek insight or understanding. When you feel you are missing context or you are unsure of the discussion, seek clarity by asking others "what" and "how" questions.

*If you are stressed,* ask questions and repeat the exact words you hear without emotion and then ask, "Did I understand you correctly?" or "Did I phrase that right?" Definitions and understanding of words are different. For further clarity, ask for examples: "Could you give me an example of that behavior?" or "Could you describe what you mean when you say _____?"

Maintain eye contact but take notes if possible. Try to stay objective. If questioned about what you are doing, say, "Your comments are important to me. I want to make sure I get them down correctly before responding."

---

## In seeking clarity, write down the questions you ask of yourself as well.

---

### Get clear about the fear

You may have heard the phrase "fear is false evidence appearing real." Have you ever noticed that much of what you worry about doesn't actually occur? And when something unusual does occur, you couldn't have prepared for it. To address worries and concerns, write them down or verbalize them to someone who will write them down for you exactly as you express them. Write down your worries and concerns. Then ask yourself:

- What is my *real* concern about this?
- What are my options? (There are usually several.)
- What am I choosing right now?
- When will I revisit that decision?
- What's the worst thing that can happen and can I live with that outcome?

When you see your concerns in black and white, you can decide what you want to do. Not what you are being *forced* to do, but what you *choose* to do *at this time.* Looking at each concern separately, determine whether it is an important issue to address now, if you should wait awhile, or if you want to let it go. (Remember, if you make one decision and don't like the results you receive, you can usually choose another strategy.)

**K: Know.** With the situation at hand and the information you have gained, know what you should do *next.* Know what your next-best request is. You don't have to have all the details filled in, just be clear about what is next. If you don't know what you should do next, then ask more questions to help you gain clarity.

*If you are stressed,* know what request makes the most sense right now. Do you need to ask a question to clear up a misunderstanding? Should you ask to determine which options are available to you with the news you've just been given? Is your best request a break?

### Take a break

Have you ever been surprised by a request and were lost for an answer? Don't feel you must respond immediately to new information. You may need a break to get some insight first or reflect on your response. You may suggest a break to allow others to gather their thoughts or compose themselves, especially when they are emotional.

Whether to regroup, think through new information, seek information, or just breathe, it's OK to hit the pause button. Take the break you need to process instead of rushing to respond. If you ask for a break, use it to stretch, walk outside for a moment, go to the bathroom, get a glass of water, and breathe. Ask for the time and use it to compose yourself and gather your thoughts. Ask the other person to take a break by asking.

- "Looks as if we are at a place we can take a break. Any issue with talking tomorrow morning?"
- "I'm going to need a quick break. Should we reconvene here in ten minutes?"
- "Thanks for bringing this matter to my attention. I want to respond with the same amount of thought you have put into our conversation. Can we talk tomorrow afternoon so I can look into what you are telling me?"
- "From your tone, this conversation sounds like I need to clear my calendar so we can have uninterrupted time. Can you come back this afternoon at three?"

## Sometimes you just have to walk away—
## but not as often as you might think.

### *Take a break from complainers*

Identifying a shared issue gives some relief or comfort in know-ing "I'm not alone." There are some benefits in hearing work-able strategies from others with the same challenges. Also, you can encourage and hold each other accountable when you spot blocks.

## Misery may love company, but
## busy people don't love misery.

Watch out for those who complain and then do nothing to resolve their issues. Usually, they ask for your advice but then don't take it. These negative energy drainers create excuses and well-structured reasons for why they behave as victims. Yet they take no action. They stop themselves from making requests and finding solutions. Their negative attitude is catching and unhelpful.

### *Conditioned not to ask*

Have you been conditioned not to ask? If so, your messages growing up sounded like these:

- "Do what I asked you to do without questioning me."
- "Don't be greedy. Take only what you need."
- "When I want your opinion, I'll ask for it."
- "Stop with the questions already. Just do it."
- "Why? Because I said so, that's why."

Behave, work hard, be kind, stay in line, and don't ask too many questions. Awards are given for maintaining the peace and not questioning authority. Be compliant. Do what you're told, and you could win the Good Citizenship Award, Most Likeable Student, or Miss Congeniality.

*Some cultures we work with are very hierarchical. If the boss is on the conference call, the person who knows the information or solution traditionally won't speak up. We have to pose the question to the person by name to get an answer.*

Perhaps your culture created a reluctance to ask questions or step out of your comfort zone. If so, maybe you heard words encouraging you to:

- Above all, save face.
- Place others' needs before yours.
- Respect order and rules.
- Children should be seen, not heard.
- Don't interrupt elders.
- Don't make waves. Respect tradition.
- Protect our family name from shame and embarrassment.

Maybe religion conditioned you not to ask. Most religions share themes of humility, rewards for the meek and the poor, waiting patiently, avoiding greed, and trusting that your needs will be taken care of and your problems solved.

Does your background have similar teachings? Surprisingly, many of the same sources (your family, culture, schools, religion, etc.) offer contradicting, positive advice that encourages you to speak up. For instance, "If you don't say something, who will?" "How will you know if you don't ask?" and "Speak now or forever hold your peace."

## Many Religions Encourage Asking

Books of faith and religious teaching often encourage asking questions. Integral in Buddhist meditation is the art of questioning and truth inquiry. Islam teaches that "We should not hesitate to ask Him [Allah] over and over again ... because that is the closest that we are to Him."

Judaism encourages learning and asking questions from the youngest person to the oldest. For example, in *The Haggadah*, the text used at the Passover holiday dinner, four questions are essential to retelling the story of the Jews' Exodus from Egypt. In the New Testament of the Bible, there are several passages on asking in order to receive, including one with an "Ask" acronym: <u>A</u>sk <u>S</u>eek <u>K</u>nock: "<u>A</u>sk and it will be given to you; <u>s</u>eek and you will find; <u>k</u>nock and the door will be opened to you. For everyone who asks receives; the one who seeks finds; and to the one who knocks, the door will be opened." Matthew 7:7-8 (emphasis added)

When you stop yourself from making a request, ask yourself, "Where did that come from? Can I find any other message that follows my values and would serve me better now?"

### Banish Blocks

Beliefs and behaviors designed to keep you safe in the past as a child or young adult can stop or block you from requesting what is possible today. Those self-limiting beliefs may not be applicable to the life you are now leading. When your beliefs no longer serve you, you may unintentionally self-sabotage and prevent yourself from requesting what you want.

*My inner saboteur says that I'm not worth it.*

Unless addressed, self-limiting beliefs and behaviors continue to expand and become a self-limiting *reality*. You have a choice. You can wait to outgrow your blocks or you can use breakthrough strategies to accelerate the process. Much like a writer's block, an asking block keeps you stuck without options or the perception of only bad choices.

### Blocks don't just disappear with awareness

You've read the comments in which people said, "I don't have an issue with asking." Knowledge that others ask without hesitation can be aggravating and demotivating. *Recognizing* you have a block doesn't remove it. Neither does:

- Intense reflection about how illogical you are.
- Telling yourself that smart people shouldn't block their own success.
- Comparing yourself with others.
- Thinking, "Well, it could be worse ..."

Sorry. Beating yourself up doesn't work. Smart people often think they can solve their asking limitations with education and by acquiring more information. High achievers add pressure thinking they should know how to ask or behave in a certain way. Further, if you are compensated to solve problems or make decisions, you may ask yourself, "How can people pay me for my wisdom and thinking when I can't solve my own issues?" Sherry Buffington, director of Quantim Leap University, explains that over time you grow more frustrated while the block remains and even gains strength:

Every self-limiting belief blocking your progress serves a purpose. Until you understand that and find a healthier way to

fulfill that purpose, nothing you do will make much difference. Even the strongest desire and the most heroic effort
will not eliminate a self-limiting belief as long as what you
desire consciously is in conflict with the subconscious reason
for maintaining it.

If you are willing to do things differently and even risk being
uncomfortable for a short time to eliminate or manage your
block, you can dramatically increase your long-term results.
Instead of ignoring or avoiding the fear or inaction, use the ASK
Strategy.

**Aware:**
- "I feel stress regarding _____."
- "I'm stalling on _____."

**Seek Clarity:**
- "What are my options?"
- "What's the worst thing that could happen?"
- "How could I be blocking myself?"

**Know Your Next-Best Request:**
- "With what I know, what makes the most sense right now?"
- "What would a Master Requester do?"
- "If I knew I couldn't fail, what outrageous ask would I
  make?"

### Fear of the past

Hesitation to ask can result from a bad experience in your history. Instead of concentrating on the *different* challenge you have
before you *today*, you dwell on what went wrong in the past. You
avoid facing something that seems similar. Being wary makes
sense. Any sane person wants to guard against repeating a bad
result.

---

**You can choose to live in the past—
or choose to live past it. Make peace with
your past before it tears you to pieces.**

---

### Overcome your past

Stop reliving past mistakes you made. You aren't perfect. That is great news because perfect people aren't much fun. Remember:

- You've had bad surprises, but you've also had pleasant ones.
- Most mistakes are fixable. You've survived the last several.
- You have learned from the past. If you make a mistake, what actions would you take *now* that you didn't know how to do *then*?

If you made a mistake or someone didn't grant your request in the past, let it go. Today is a new day, with new people who don't know that you made a mistake five years ago. Make the best request you can for now. You can adjust if needed.

### Flo

Flo grew up in a dysfunctional family. Her dad traveled and her mom struggled with some emotional issues. At twelve, Flo's responsibilities included cooking, grocery shopping, and managing the home, including taking care of her younger brothers and sister. Despite the turmoil, Flo made good grades, received a college scholarship, and landed a good job as a supervisor. When Flo notices that she's stalling to have a disciplinary conversation with an employee, she asks herself, "I wonder why I'm holding back. Although this situation isn't pleasant, I'm an adult. This is not the chaos I grew up in. As his manager, I need to let my employee know that his performance has negative effects on our team. He may not like the feedback, but he needs to address the behavior before it gets worse and impacts his career."

## Get rid of the head garbage.

### *Proof of breakthroughs*

Do you recognize any past beliefs you had but no longer hold? If so, those breakthroughs are proof you can overcome your self-limiting beliefs and behavior.

> *I was afraid of looking stupid or embarrassing myself fifteen years ago as my younger self. But once I turned thirty-five, I stopped worrying. I'm so glad not to be young anymore. I'm so much wiser now and realize that if I want something changed, my request is probably reasonable.*

 **Lead to Ask**

Good leaders, mentors, and coaches know that high performance relies on more than providing proper training and tools to do the job. Strengthening the ability to problem solve and to focus often requires managing distracting mental roadblocks. Discuss these block questions. For a worksheet to help you walk through the blocks with those you lead, go to AskOutrageously.com.

### Outrageous Review

- An asking block keeps you stuck without options, just like a writer's block prevents a writer from writing. Identify your blocks. Then focus on determining how that belief or behavior is limiting you.
- Feeling nervous or scared when you are getting ready to ask is a normal response. It causes you to be hyper-focused on your behavior. Use it to your advantage.

- When you are unsure about facing a difficult conversation, use the ASK Strategy.
- High achievers internalize the pressure to know all the answers. Don't let that block hold you back from asking.
- When making requests, resist the urge to concentrate on a bad experience you've had in the past or when your request was denied. Instead, focus on the challenge you have in front of you today, at this very moment.
- Developing a good habit requires practice. Practice asking for what you want at safe places such as grocery stores, garage sales, flea markets, and restaurants. Make asking become a habit.

 **Smart Asks**

- What past beliefs do I no longer hold?
- When I feel nervous, how can I use the energy to help me focus?
- How can I stay more aware of the situation at hand?
- What questions will help me get more information?
- How can I remind myself to focus on my next-best request?

 **Ask List**

*Trash your block.* Rid yourself of the head garbage, *literally.* On a piece of paper, write down whatever issue is blocking you from asking for what you want. Then mentally tell yourself, "That's trash talk. This belief or behavior might have served me once, but I don't need it anymore." Next, wad up the paper in a tight ball, and throw that outdated belief in the trash can where it belongs. In the future, if you find yourself blocking a request, remember you have a *new* response.

## Secret Success Tools

The best way to solve an asking block and make more impactful requests requires *asking* for help. Download the "Spot Your Asking Block" and "Knock Your Asking Block" activities as well as instructions from the tools and resources page on AskOutrageously.com.

# Eight

# Asking for Others

You may be great at asking for others, but not yourself. Two-thirds of people in the Ask Outrageously Study reported they are more comfortable asking on behalf of someone else—such as a client, a cause, a child, or a person in their care—than asking for themselves (see Figure 8). This is no surprise. It is easier to summon the courage and risk embarrassment when you request for those who rely on you.

You may have been conditioned by your family, school, community, or place of worship to think of others first. Maybe you learned that asking for what you want or asking for more than "your share" is selfish or reflects a flaw in your character.

In a culture that encourages sensitivity, respect, and good manners, people teach themselves to compromise, make do, settle for less, and not make waves.

When asking for someone else, you still face the same risk of getting a no, yet it's considerably less unpleasant. Study participants shared why.

*It is easier to support someone else than it is to talk about myself.*

*The stakes simply are lower because it's for someone else.*

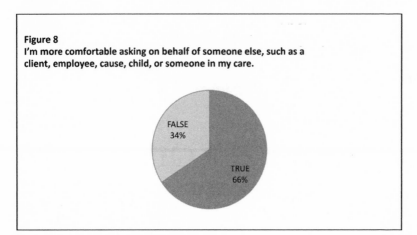

**Figure 8**
**I'm more comfortable asking on behalf of someone else, such as a client, employee, cause, child, or someone in my care.**

*It's easier if the request does not benefit me in any way.*

*Supporting the underdog is easier.*

*It's less personal and not as disappointing if I am told no.*

*It does not feel selfish to ask for others. I'm not as adventurous in asking for things I personally want because I don't feel entitled.*

Notice how these comments are focused on the feelings and views of the person asking—and not on the person being asked. Many of the remaining third of the people in the study reported they were comfortable making a request whether they were the person who *benefited* or not. A few respondents did state that people should ask for themselves; their belief was that people who received the benefit should ask.

*If a person is capable, then that person should be asking.*

*They should ask. They know more about their situations than I do.*

*If there is a fundraiser at school, children should call and ask me to buy whatever it is. I don't like it when they don't. They are the ones who get the benefit.*

---

**President John F. Kennedy famously said, "Ask not what your country can do for you, ask what you can do for your country."**

---

### Self-Interest versus Selfishness

One of the biggest challenges is realizing that asking for your interests doesn't mean you are selfish or trying to cheat others. You are simply attempting to get the best deal you can. Unfortunately, a common perception is that it is wrong to want an outcome for yourself.

*People will assume I'm greedy.*

*I don't ask because I'm afraid people will think I'm taking advantage of them.*

You often see the same types of concerns or reluctance when people are having difficulties in sales. People don't want to appear greedy, undesirable, or too manipulative. They don't want to be an inconvenience, so they don't inform others of what they want.

### Ask for others

One possible solution when you are reluctant to make requests on your own behalf is to think about who your request benefits other than yourself.

- When you take a risk and ask a question in class, you are helping the other students understand material they might have missed.
- When you speak up at an intimidating board meeting, the answer you receive often helps other members of the group with an important decision.

- If you ask for a bonus or a raise you are due, you benefit your family with extra money to pay bills or take a vacation.

You can take the same passion and drive to ask for others and apply it to meeting your own needs. Again, the great majority of people in the study (two-thirds) said they feel more comfortable asking when it benefits another. People do heroic acts for children, those they love, and causes they feel passionate about. They make outrageous requests without any intimidation or hesitation.

### Individual requests

When it comes to individuals or causes they care about, many people are passionate and fearless. They ask outrageously without hesitation when their efforts benefit a cause greater than themselves or their own organization.

### Pat

A business professor and master requester, Pat also volunteers as the PTA carnival chair at her kids' elementary school. For five years she has found donations and purchased prizes for the annual carnival. Pat is born to do this role and is gutsy in her requests. She locates toys, games, and coloring books on sale. Then she asks the store manager to request better pricing:"Hi, I'm Pat. I'm the Dartmouth Elementary PTA carnival chair. I see you have a lot of coloring books for a dollar. These pallets take up a lot of floor space. Would you lower your price to five cents apiece if I took them all?"

At times Pat hears, "No. They are already discounted as much as I'm allowed." Sometimes she hears, "How about ten cents or fifty cents?" More often than not, she hears, "Great. I'll help you load them. Where's your vehicle?"

### Gloria

Gloria is a member of a non-profit organization that meets nightly in a local building. Recently, city inspectors deemed the building a danger to the safety of its occupants and the public. Seeing options, Gloria approaches an entrepreneur who owns other properties in the community. She asks if he "knows of anyone who has a building available for nightly meetings." The owner identifies several other property owners who have buildings and recommends one or two to call. He then expresses further interest in the organization. Gloria shares the group's mission and programs. At the end of their conversation, he suggests Gloria approach the non-profit's leaders to ask if they are willing to enter into a long-term contract. If the leaders agree, he will commit to *purchasing* a building for the organization with the understanding that they will lease the property from him at a greatly reduced rate for five years. Needless to say, Gloria is surprised at the response and interest shown by the entrepreneur.

### Greta

Greta feels moved by a recent disaster in Asia. Right now her funds are limited, but she can donate $500. By asking her co-workers, she finds others who want to donate. And one of her team members tells her that the human resources department will coordinate a company match. Greta's $500 grows into a $3,000 donation almost overnight through her requests.

Your ask can grow exponentially. Ask others to participate in programs like GoFundMe and Benevolent. You expand support for your cause from people you know to people you may have never met. You can use these programs to crowdsource their contribution. Be bold. Make the request for support.

## Ask locally

Community efforts create opportunities to practice asking others to donate their time, talents, and treasure. In turn, those who donate know that the recipients have been evaluated and their contributions are managed to provide maximum benefit. Request ways to expand efforts in your community.

- Ask residents if they want to collaborate on a community service project such as revitalizing a neighborhood or volunteer at a local food bank.
- Ask local citizens if they want to participate in a cleanup project or a walk to bring awareness to a disease.
- Ask the business next door if the owner wants to cooperate and play a part in your special event sale.
- Ask a small business owner if he or she would like to put coupons in your event swag bag or donate items for a silent auction.
- Ask neighboring businesses if they would like to give free services to drive donations for a cause and bring awareness to their personal services business.
- Ask city officials to come and see your new neighborhood developments. Visits generate interest and help the permission process go more smoothly.

### Artie

Artie Williams is the director of marketing and development for a local emergency clinic. He looks for appropriate sponsorship opportunities to partner with in the community. Artie asks the local high school cheerleading squad if they can participate in the clinic's grand opening. The team performs a special cheer at the opening and promotes the new clinic through their community's social media. In turn, the clinic gives the team a large donation that helps sponsor the team's annual pink T-shirt campaign to fight breast cancer.

### Non-profit requests

Requests are the lifeblood of foundations and non-profits. How would you raise money if you didn't sell or provide services? Charitable organizations face this challenge daily. In addition to methods like individual donations, corporate contributions, and asking for grants, there are creative ways to ask for funding and provide a benefit for their donors:

- Planned giving as part of estate planning including bequest, gift annuity, trust, life insurance policy, or real estate
- Companies matching employees' or retirees' contributions
- Stock donation
- In-kind gifts such as computers, equipment, furniture, or air miles
- Donor's name added to buildings, gardens, meeting areas, or bricks
- Giving days that allow organizations to participate in a matching fund
- School alumni donations of money, time, mentoring, and land

Mellanie True Hills, founder and CEO of StopAfib.org and American Foundation for Women's Health, offers this advice:

> When making a grant request, ask as much as you can of them to learn about the process and the organization's priorities, but also understand that they may not be able to share much with you, especially in a highly regulated space. If you know someone who has experience in that space or industry with grant requests, work with the person to improve your chances of success.

## Wintegrity

Consider who else can benefit when you ask for yourself. People want to be a part of something bigger than themselves. They want to feel good about their efforts and positively impact the world. If all parties involved can "win" and do it with high standards and integrity, you have "wintegrity."

The practice of wintegrity works with everyone from an employee and boss to a client and a teenager. When people help create or build a solution they believe is "right" with people they trust, it is far more likely to be a solution that lasts and offers a bigger reach. Organizations practice wintegrity when they ask how their operations can also positively impact the community or the world.

---

### *Together, we win the right way.*
**Employee Value Proposition,
Hewlett Packard Enterprises**

---

Companies are finding that the more they invest in their communities, the more customers and employees invest in them. Starbucks, Origins, and Whole Foods are examples of companies that ask their customers to pay more in order to benefit others. They are profitable, and they attract and retain employees.

### *Tim*

Tim McCarthy and his wife, Alice, created The Business of Good Foundation, a non-profit that shares business knowledge with other non-profits. Tim asks other organizations to partner with them to fund investments and to offer best practices from the business sector to those who serve the poor. In exchange, businesses learn how to expand their social impact through the non-profit sector.

As chief mission officer of the foundation, Tim explains, "Requests become a virtuous cycle. Our restaurant business is fed by the interest of our community in us, and so as we become known for our genuine interest in them, our business grows organically."

### Asks of kindness

You've probably heard of acts of random kindness. People anonymously do nice things for strangers. They pay for coffee for the person in line behind them. They donate clothes to a family in need. Perhaps they put extra money in a meter to help someone avoid a ticket. These kind people consciously make someone else's day in an unexpected way.

Asks of kindness are similar. However, instead of remaining anonymous, you intentionally connect. You probably practice asks of kindness and aren't aware of the effect. When you ask, you increase the benefit people receive by allowing them the dignity to decide how you can help them.

## Are you aware of the influence you have?

Betty Garrett, author of *From Chaos to Control*, says, "People want to help you when you or a loved one is ill. They aren't sure what you need." She suggests making a list of things to give to others when they ask what they can do. "People ask if you need anything. Help them know what to ask." Betty's *Share the Load: Meaningful Ways You Can Offer to Help* is located in the Resources section on AskOutrageously.com.

### Practice asks of kindness

Asking improves lives. The proof is revealed every time you ask and people accept your kindness. Your efforts show the power you possess to make a difference with a simple request. More importantly, you feel grateful for your ability to help others.

- Ask people who are waiting in line to purchase tickets for an event if they would like your extra seats at no cost.
- Ask traveling military personnel if you can buy their snacks, meals, drinks, or headsets, or insist they trade places with you and take your upgraded seats.
- Ask someone new to your company if he or she would like to have lunch and meet some people who work in other departments.
- Ask a person if you can get the door for them, or reach an item on a shelf for someone who is shorter or in a wheelchair.
- Ask a teacher if he needs some help with his class or a child if she needs box tops for her school organization.
- Ask a neighbor who lives alone to join you at a function, movie, or church service.
- Ask working parents if they need something from the store or if you can watch the children while they run errands.
- Ask a person who is injured or sick if you could mow the lawn or pick up dinner.

### Bunny

When Bunny Summerlin was hired as the director of the Metrocrest Services Agency, she asked the clients how they best needed to be helped. In response, Bunny created a shopping experience at the annual holiday store. Clients could shop with dignity on a point system. Volunteers now asked how the shoppers would like to be served. "The old way didn't make sense," Bunny said. "We were giving every girl a doll and every boy a ball. Our clients know their family members' needs. They know who needs gifts and what is appropriate. We just needed to ask them."

And accept offers to help you. If *you* experience joy and a feeling of gratitude when people accept your request to help, doesn't it make sense that others will experience similar feelings if they can help you? They will. You deny others the joy of being of service when you don't make requests. Not only is it kind to ask others if you can help them, it is kind to ask them for help and accept their offer to help you.

###  Lead Others to Ask

Ask someone you lead to pick a teambuilding event to benefit a non-profit. Ask that person to recruit others for a planning team, then lead the organization's efforts and make the requests. Discuss how the experience relates to requests at work.

### Outrageous Review

- Winning with wintegrity means you are requesting a solution that benefits all parties with trust and honesty. A solution based on wintegrity builds relationships and has longer-lasting effects because the parties are less likely to renege on the agreement.

- The majority of people (two-thirds, according to the Ask Outrageously Study) are more likely to be comfortable asking on behalf of someone else instead of themselves. Use this to your advantage by framing the situation about who else your requests will benefit, for example:

    "If I ask for a raise, then my family will benefit from the ability to pay more bills."
    "If I ask this question in class, then everyone else will understand what the teacher is saying."

"If I ask for a donation for a local fundraiser, then the community will benefit."

"If I ask for a financial gift from a corporate donor, then cancer patients will benefit from the medical research the donation funds."

## Smart Asks

- Am I acting with wintegrity or just trying to please others?
- How can I ask to help or be of service to someone else?
- Am I practicing random "asks of kindness" to help or be of service to others?
- When I make my next request, who else benefits if I'm successful?

## Ask List

- Ask a traveling member of the military if you can buy a meal or insist that he or she trade places with you and take your upgraded seat.
- Ask a sick coworker if you can help cover his or her workload for the day.
- Hold doors open for others.
- Make one outrageous request for yourself that also benefits someone else.

## Secret Success Tools

Download "Share the Load: Meaningful Ways You Can Offer to Help" in *From Chaos to Control: A Survival Guide for the Cancer Caregiver* by Betty Garrett. Watch "The World Needs You to Ask Outrageously" from SMU/TEDx on AskOutrageously. com.

# Nine

# Authority

When possible, make your requests to people who can make decisions. Asking those in authority can make some people feel insecure. These requesters are apprehensive about differences in wealth, training, age, or gender. They believe their education, experience, or upbringing has not prepared them to talk to those who wield power. Do you hesitate when making requests of those in authority? If so, you're not alone—several survey respondents do:

*I dread the repercussions of asking.*

*Asking may cause even more work for me without a guaranteed positive outcome.*

*If I ask, the other person might expect favors in return.*

*The person I need to ask is an intimidating person, which makes me uncomfortable in asking.*

A difference in experience or education can be daunting. For example, professors and teachers have authority positions that intimidate many. In the survey, 28 percent of respondents reported that they would *never* talk to their professor about a grade or ask for a grade change. Why wouldn't you see a teacher about your grade? The teacher knows the reason you didn't get the grade you expected. You could receive help in understanding a concept or get clarification or ideas to try next time. Also, teachers are human. They may have made mistakes. Lorri Allen, a university journalism professor, explains:

> As a teacher and adviser, I don't understand why only one or two students come to my office each semester. When my students ask for help, they receive a lot of extra one-on-one time. And I'm a better teacher if students ask because I know their issues. I'm impressed by their willingness to go to the trouble of asking. Those who ask for help always end up making better grades than they would have otherwise.

On the subject of education, parents and caregivers often aren't sure how to ask teachers about grades or for recommendations. The best questions a parent or caregiver can ask a teacher when a child's performance is less than desirable are:

> "I've noticed my child's grades have dropped recently. Has she come in for help?"

> "Do you have any recommendations to support him learning at home?"

> "Are you noticing any unusual behavior?"

"Parents should ask, 'Is my child doing everything within his or her control to do better or get a better result?'" suggests Mike Link, a high school orchestra teacher in McKinney, Texas.

Most people in authority *know* that you don't have their same experiences. There's no need to pretend, try to impress, or attempt to fit in. For the most part, when you ask for more information, you show an eagerness to learn and improve your understanding.

### "Them"

Don't be too impressed with "them," no matter what their roles or titles are. Important people don't have time to waste. Stop worrying how you appear or if "they" like you. When decision makers are spending their most precious commodity, their time, with you—then you have something they want.

Practice asking about and identifying the people with authority. Look for those who have the power to grant your requests. Watch these decision makers' reactions. They listen and consider requests thoughtfully. They are the problem solvers. They step in when others are stuck. Start watching for people who can and will say yes. Observe that, unless stressed, people with authority

---

### Ask to See a Manager

Nothing makes employees jump to attention faster than these words:

"May I ask to see someone in charge?"

"Is your manager around?"

Let someone in authority know about a problem you spot in his or her establishment. (For example, "I noticed your lights are out in the parking lot.") Tell the manager if the service could be improved.

Ask to see a supervisor and tell him or her about an employee who did a superior job helping you. That boss will be shocked that you're praising, not complaining.

aren't offended by requests. When they say no, they often make a counteroffer or educate you on their reasoning.

### Checking for authority

Do not offend the people you are connecting with by asking if they are able to make decisions. Often, people play an important role in the process and carry your request to those who make the final decisions. Instead, use questions to determine who has authority to grant your request.

"Who besides yourself will be involved in making this decision?"

"How do you like to receive information?"

"Can you walk me through your decision-making process?"

If you can identify the people who are involved in granting requests, you can ask better questions and provide better information to each person involved.

Pay attention to what your connection shares about the decision makers. Those with authority may need visuals, bottom-line recommendations, or detailed documentation to make the decision. If you can't get an audience with those in authority, equip your contact with the information they need to effectively present your request. When you prepare your messenger well, your message is more likely to be heard correctly.

## Dealing with Decision Makers

Decision makers don't mind you asking questions, especially if the answers could lead to improving their business. When you ask, they are concerned that you respect their most valuable asset, their time. By the way, if they are asking questions or answering yours, you have something they need.

Ever hear the adage "curiosity killed the cat"? Well, it's only because that cat didn't ask first. People in authority encourage curiosity. Ask questions with confidence when you're dealing with decision makers.

- What were you looking for me to help you with today?
- What do you think is really the cause of this problem?
- What do your people say is the reason for this issue?
- How big a problem is this? (Time, expense, resources?)
- How much mental energy are you spending each week on this issue?
- What happens if you do nothing?
- What has worked so far in your attempts to resolve it?
- What hasn't worked?
- How would you describe your perfect solution?
- How would you know this issue is solved?

True decision makers appreciate decisiveness and getting to the point. Most decision makers have limited time and a short attention span. Provide them bullet points, executive summaries, and a clear understanding of the type of response or the decision you are requesting. Keep your communication brief. Narrow down the facts.

*We provide our leaders with the basics of our request: Who is involved? What is needed? When it will be deployed and what problems do we anticipate? There's a skill to communicating with executives. We call it "executizing."*

### So what?
Often the question people in authority want answered is, "So what?" Meaning: "Give me the bottom line. Tell me why this is important. Show me how your request matters." Decision mak-

ers want to know the good business reasons they should grant your request.

### Daisy

To Daisy Chin-Lor, President of Tupperware & Nutrimetics for Australia & New Zealand, the questions you ask and the responses you receive are the obvious way to show you are engaged and truly interested. A global executive, Daisy has lived in seven countries and led Fortune 100 companies in direct selling, luxury retailing, and beauty products. Daisy says, "I am often faced with reams of information and analysis that justify a situation, a business proposal, or an update on a project. Much time goes into preparing the data, fact checking, and creating pretty presentations for my review. While I truly appreciate the work the preparation entails, my question always is … *So what?*" She says she often gets a blank stare. "My intention is to be more provocative and engage a conversation that digs deeper than merely charts, figures, and slides. The question translates across most cultures and sparks a real discussion or passion (or not) about the project. So what? If you don't know, you really don't care, right?"

### All talk no power

Have you come across people who don't say no but won't say yes? Instead, they are always cordial and ask for more information—pretty much stringing you along. They are "all talk and no go." These time wasters may offer to help you with a project but are unusually busy the two weeks you need their help. The introductions they promise never materialize. If you are working in sales or a customer-facing role, these lurkers will let you take them to lunch or golfing. Every now and then, they'll ask for a favor or pump you for information, but they never buy or make a decision. Eventually you realize you're dealing with an excuse maker and staller, not an influencer or a decision maker.

## The powerless only have the power to say no.

Most aren't intentionally using you, but they don't have the authority to say yes. However, treat them with respect. Going around the proverbial gatekeeper can get you barred from any future discussions. Not following protocol can ruin your chances of getting a yes. Similarly, jumping over *your* boss's head to ask for something could make them mad and minimize your chances of being taken seriously.

> *If the answer is no, I always say, "It seems that you are unable to say yes or help me, so who can I talk to who would be able to say yes or help me?"*

The powerless continually ask for more information but can't tell you when a decision will be made. People who have to constantly double-check or delay with vague or illogical reasons *aren't* the decision makers. Waiting for the person who is able to make a decision is well-invested time.

### No mind reading

Master requesters don't make their requests in a vacuum, relying only on their own research. They test their suspicions by asking other people questions for clarification. Instead of guessing, they ask other people what is important. The old adage "people will support what they help build" works in asking as well. Let others help build or participate in the solution by using these questions:

- "If you could get everything you wanted, what would you want to see happen?"
- "What would be a win for you here?"

### Past asks

Smart people find out what other people have asked for or done. If they can't determine this information on their own, they request the information from others. Here's what to ask:

- "You've made several requests like this one. What information do people usually ask you to provide?"
- "What do people in my position usually ask from people like you?"

### Ask deeper

Experts who ask for what they really want share several traits. Instead of *working* harder, they *ask* smarter and with questions that go deeper. They ask open-ended questions, listen to the answers, and then use follow-up questions to clarify, such as "Can you tell me more?" and "What else?" They don't pretend to be mind readers. Instead, they ask, pause, and let others fill in the blanks.

- "What is important for you to tell me before beginning? *Anything else?*"
- "What have you seen tried in the past that works? *Can you say more?*"

---

**Ask and let others fill in the blanks with their information.**

---

### Help solving your issues

You can't know the detailed operation of others' organizations, teams, or even families. Instead of making assumptions, tell the other party your concerns and ask for help in solving them.

- "One of the concerns I have is obtaining access to the people and data needed to solve this issue. What ideas do you have to make those people and that information available?"
- "Communication has been an issue in the past, especially with calendaring. What do you recommend to keep everyone on the same page?"
- "What objections do you think your employees might have? What's the best plan to address those concerns?"

### Don't pretend to know

Decision makers can spot someone who is pretending or stalling. Don't pretend to know all the answers. Instead, prepare to the extent you can. When your request is met with a question you can't answer, it is OK to say, "I don't know." Ask whether the answer is needed before you can move forward:

- "I have no idea. How important is that information in making your decision?"
- "I don't know. The question hasn't come up before. Would you like me to find out the answer or should we proceed?"

Instead of promising to check on it and bring back an answer, first make sure the information is important. Don't waste your time unnecessarily researching answers that won't be used in making a decision.

Don't be consumed with the right questions being asked the right way at precisely the right time. That's too overwhelming. You aren't following a script. Ask and then listen before asking again. Being heard is a gift. Most people will respect your efforts to listen to their answers. And the more they talk, the more you learn. You know your request and your reasons to support it. Even when responding to their questions, keep the focus on them.

## Answer Then Ask

When it is your turn to speak, be prepared to answer similar questions posed to you. Then direct the focus back to them by asking a question.

- "What I want is _____."
  (Describe your desired result. Then ask, "What is your perfect scenario?")
- "What's important for me to know is _____."
  (Answer. Then ask, "What about you?")
- "What I've tried that worked well was _____."
  ("What have you tried?")
- "If it is OK with you, what I think should happen next is _____.
  ("What do you think our next step should be?")
- "I can identify several areas we should discuss are _____
  _____.
  (Offer an idea. Then ask, "What needs to be added?")
- "I can answer a few of your questions right now, but several we need to explore are _____."
  (Identify any questions. Then ask, "What else did you want?")

## You Need Help

You can't do it all by yourself. In this age of collaboration, you can't say, "I don't need to ask for help. I'll figure it out by myself." Nope. In a land of school project partnering, work teams, flashmobs, and crowdsourcing, participation is the key. Self-starters are recognized, but self-sufficiency is no longer appreciated or encouraged. Peggy Collins, author of *Help Is Not a Four-Letter Word*, offers this advice:

> Make a point to ask for help when the occasion arises. It might be frightening at first to hand over control to someone else if you are self-sufficient or usually make all the decisions. However, when you incorporate other people in creating a plan, the chance of an outright rejection is minimized. Your loss of control is not absolute. And there is a feeling of camaraderie. That's a win/win.

### Raj

Raj works in a competitive environment where there is pressure to perform or risk termination. Raj recently received feedback that his "deliverables aren't on schedule," and he "must stop doing all the work himself." Raj doesn't ask others because he fears they won't do the work right or might make mistakes. Raj tells himself, "I know I worry about doing it right or losing my job. However, I'm never going to complete what is needed unless I delegate. To make sure the work meets my standards, I'll ask the right people to help and put a communication plan in place. Also, we need to develop a schedule with touchpoints to ensure the timelines are hit and the quality is where it needs to be."

### Request support

To command more influence and strengthen your ability to make requests at the highest levels, consider forming or joining a peer advisory group. People establish these groups to support each other's efforts, challenge each other to grow, and obtain better results. The members become your personal board of directors and you are theirs. Some peer advisory groups are created through a formal structure and are designed to bring together professionals with similar roles in different organizations. For instance, formal peer advisory groups for chief executives include Vistage, the Executive Women's Forum, The Alternative Board (TAB), Women's Professional Organization (WPO) and YPO, formerly the Young Presidents' Organization.

Other peer advisory groups have a more informal structure based on the needs of their members. You may want to form your own advisory or mastermind group. The insights and ability gained in collaborating with people interested in growth will shortcut your learning and help you avoid pitfalls. The accountability, feedback, and support are priceless.

*Our accountability team has conducted a weekly check-in call for the past two weeks since the retreat. Our basic agenda is (a) what have you accomplished, (b) who have you tried to reconnect with? and (c) what do you need help with? We keep it concise, but also have time to talk about what we need.*

Create your own cheerleading squad of people you trust and who believe in you. Ask people you respect to breakfast, lunch, or an after-work event. You will be surprised at who will say yes. People want to connect when they are given the opportunity.

### Diamonds

Michelle, Susan, and Alysen wanted to meet other women at similar levels of professional success who worked in different industries and companies. They asked other high-powered businesswomen to commit their time and energy to support each other. Recognizing they are all works in progress, they called themselves the Diamonds, short for "diamonds in the rough." Diamonds attend each other's speeches, support causes, meet for happy hour, and advise each other. Want to guess how you gain entry and hang out with these power women? By *asking*. Someone has to ask or invite you.

 **Lead to Ask**

Ask those you lead and coach to meet someone from a different department or a different organization for coffee or lunch. Ask your employees to attend a strategic meeting with you or, when appropriate, attend in your place. Ask them to consider their objectives before attending and to watch for requests made. Have them report their observations to their coworkers.

**Outrageous Review**
- A perceived lack of education or experience, differences in upbringing, or differences in wealth prevent people from asking for what they want. They fear that if they ask questions of someone with higher status/authority that person may lose respect for them or repercussions could occur.
- Asking outrageously doesn't mean going around others or asking over their heads. Breaching protocol or insulting a lower-ranking person who isn't the real decision maker will often kill your chances of success.
- Watch out for the powerless, who will never say yes to your request. These time wasters and lurkers will be cordial, offer to help, and give all the signals they are interested in you or your services because they can't say no. But they can't say yes either.
- Stay curious. You aren't a mind reader. It is OK to ask, "What's the best way for us to discuss this issue?" or "What would you like to see happen here?"

### Smart Asks

- What am I allowing to get in my way of asking? (Are you insecure about your education, economic status, or even your appearance?)

- Am I concerned about how I appear or if I'm liked? (Stop worrying. If decision makers are spending their most precious commodity with you, their time, then you have something they want.)

- Who is wasting my time making promises but not delivering?

### Ask List

- Ask to see store managers and give them positive or negative feedback about your shopping experience.

- If you usually agree to activities, tell people that you can't volunteer or attend an event you don't want to attend. (How does it feel? You are such a rebel!)

- Go shop for leaders. Look around and see if you can find people with the authority to make decisions.

- Invite a group of leaders or high performers you would like to know better to have lunch or breakfast. Consider meeting regularly and helping each other make better requests and decisions. Get feedback from people invested in each other's success.

### Secret Success Tools

Download "Tips for Starting a Mastermind or Peer Advisory Group" from AskOutrageously.com.

# Ten

# Tailor Your Ask

The more you know about people, the better you can connect. Ask people about their lives, their background, their work, and their interests. Their answers provide insight into how they think, the choices they make, the way they process information, and what matters to them.

When making requests of others, consider what communication style will work best. Watch how people respond. When you spot a strong preference for communication style, you have the ability to tailor your approach. When you understand a person's tendency to be more logical or more relational, extroverted or introverted, you are better able to communicate and to form relationships.

## One style of asking does not fit all.

When it comes to communicating and making requests, one size does not fit all. Although requests often involve similar facts, figures, and organizations, they involve different people who communicate differently.

## Stay Curious

When you are communicating, stay curious about what works with each person as you interact. Observe his or her language and temperament.

- Whom do you have better relationships with?
- Is small talk needed, or is it frowned upon?
- Do you need to stick to facts and prepare to address details?
- How important are summaries, bullet points, and showing the bottom line?
- Who prefers you to keep it light and upbeat?
- Do they need time to reflect, or do they like to make quick decisions?

*When I ask how they are doing, don't give me this feel-good, intangible stuff. I have to know their numbers and their metrics.*

Knowing how to connect and communicate quickly, no matter the person, greatly improves your ability to ask. Remind yourself that *everyone* is a little different than you are. Think of your family, especially brothers or sisters. They had a similar upbringing, ate the same food, grew up in the same neighborhood, and attended the same schools. Do they think or communicate differently than you do? Probably. Even identical twins choose to develop different styles, traits, and talents.

## The DEAL Strategy

To quickly assess how people prefer to be asked, use the DEAL Strategy. Do they like to:

Decide
Engage
Accommodate
Leverage

### Deciders

Deciders are serious and effective. They are action oriented and like to make decisions. They are focused on the big picture and want to quickly determine the bottom line. Deciders like questions that challenge them and make them think of choices.

What doesn't work: A lot of chitchat with unnecessary details. Don't waste their time.

Ask right away and then back up your ask with succinct and supportive details. Use logic instead of emotion. Deciders seek authority roles. If you have a big ask with a decision maker, revisit the section on Dealing with Decision Makers (page 142).

Try these deciding questions:

- "If you could address anything today, what would it be?"
- "How will you know if you are successful?"

### Engagers

Engagers are outgoing and connect well with people. Fun and relationship driven, they empower others and want to inspire and encourage as well as connect. Engagers are often the life of the party or the most exciting, entertaining people in the room.

What doesn't work: Boring facts and serious information with no connection to people.

Ask them to be creative and think of ideas that will inspire others. Engagers invent solutions and ways to communicate when no one else can.

Try these engaging questions:

- "What are some creative ideas that might lighten the mood around here?"
- "How are we going to communicate this dry material in a way that is engaging and fun?"

### Accommodators

Accommodators are usually pleasant, approachable, and agreeable. They consider if the request benefits people and if the approach is respectful and considerate.

What doesn't work: Treating them or those around them with disrespect. Don't go around them or jump protocol or you'll burn this bridge.

Ask how they believe a request will affect others. Accommodators instinctively know how people will feel or what else others need. Try these accommodating questions:

- "How is the news of the change affecting people's attitudes?"
- "What would you do to begin recognizing the efforts of others?"

### Leveragers

Leveragers are good with systems and processes and like to learn. They are more likely to say yes if the request is based on facts supported by thoughtful consideration of the best solution, and if it can be leveraged to improve efficiency.

What doesn't work: Quick requests that rush the examination process or disregard the systems in place. Undefined questions that aren't clear about the information you need.

Ask specific questions and give them time to consider your thought-out plan. Leveragers want to compare their thinking with yours. Ask them to explain how they believe the request can be implemented most effectively.

Try these leveraging questions:

- "What would be the best way to make sure you have all the information needed?"
- "When you think through the projects that were imple-

mented correctly, what were the tools used to measure them?"

Note: There are many assessments with different names for similar traits. For a chart that translates the DEAL styles into an assessment style you are familiar with, see the Resources section or go online to AskOutrageously.com.

### Introversion and Extroversion
A person's tendency to be more introverted or extroverted should be considered in your communications, especially when making requests.

### *Introversion*
Two of the DEAL styles have introversion traits: Accommodator and Leverager. In the Ask Outrageously Study, several participants said introversion was a problem for them when making requests. Their comments had a similar theme. They would rather take what was given than ask for more.

*I'm introverted and hate to bother people. These traits make it difficult for me to ask others for anything.*

*A born introvert, I've always had too much concern about how others perceive me. I'd often rather live in my own discomfort than make someone else feel the least bit uncomfortable by asking them for something.*

*I'm an introvert and have difficulty asking anyone for anything. I'm actually more comfortable not getting what I could ask for if it means I don't have to ask for it.*

People who are more introverted will often make requests privately. They may not speak up in a meeting but come to you alone after the meeting to voice concerns or ask for direction. Consider how you can talk privately to find out true interests.

### Extroversion

Two of the DEAL styles have Extroversion: Decider and Engager. People who are more extroverted generally don't have difficulties making requests but might need help when focusing on all the people or details involved. They feel comfortable speaking up in meetings and may dominate with unrelated questions.

> *Unless it's offensive or bothersome or puts the other person out, I believe people like to help people. I do. So, I ask.*

> *Why would you sit in silence and not ask? Nobody can read your mind.*

> *At times, I just go for it and ask for forgiveness after the fact.*

Bold extroverts making requests can remind you of actors performing on a stage. They process their ideas out loud and revise them in real time. Ask them for their firm commitment. If they ask a sensitive question in front of others, be prepared to say, "I'm not prepared to talk about that right now. Let's stick with what we came here to do."

Each DEAL request style has advantages as well as stumbling blocks. In each example below, someone received feedback that pertained to his or her DEAL style. Observe how each used his or her style to modify and upgrade future requests.

### Decide

Dominic likes selling. He likes to help people make decisions. However, he is leaving money on the table. He rushes to close business instead of thoroughly exploring what serves his client the best. His leader challenges him to conduct a more comprehensive needs analysis and provide his clients with customized solutions. Dominic decides to ask more in-depth questions and listen closer to his clients' challenges and objectives. Asking more questions takes more time. Dominic's speed of reaching agreements does decline. However, his decision to add questions about his clients' real needs dramatically increases the amount of his sales and his margins as well as his paycheck.

### Engage

Elise learns she is invited to attend and present at an association conference in Florence, Italy. When Elise asks her boss for approval, he reminds her that the company is restricting travel expenses. He encourages Elise to find a way to relate the travel to revenue-generating opportunities. Elise modifies her request and proposes the event as an opportunity to engage and promote the company on a global scale. In particular, she identifies potential partners who are attending and the global prospects with which she can schedule meetings and connect.

### Accommodate

Adam leads the customer service department. Adam needs to promote at least three people to handle the increased volume of calls and to accommodate current business needs and hire their replacements. His coach believes his past requests were denied because Adam was too accommodating. She asks how he might be more assertive.

Adam modifies his request to accommodate the leadership's need for documentation showing how the bottom line will be affected. He reveals how both the retention of current customers and the potential for additional sales to existing customers can increase with more help. Adam asks by accommodating the interests of all involved.

### Leverage

LeAnn's mentor helps her recognize that she is missing key opportunities to advance by not requesting leadership roles. Because of her need to think over and reflect before deciding, LeAnn missed out on three projects she could have offered to lead. This paralysis by analysis is stalling her career advancement. LeAnn considers the upcoming projects and the leadership opportunities involved in each. At the next meeting, LeAnn is first to request one of the projects. And she also comes prepared with a second project to request in case her first request isn't granted. She leverages her ability to research and her knowledge of procedures to prepare her best requests.

### Business Dealings with Different DEAL Styles

Although you may prefer certain communication styles, people often do business with people who have *different* styles. Respecting differences helps your requests get granted. Connecting with people who have different styles or motivators is the sign of a strong communicator. When making high-stakes requests, professionals often get better results when the other person has an approach that's different from theirs.

### Lars

During the annual sales conference, Lars looks around at the 150 attendees and is disappointed that so many seem disengaged. Lars jumps to his feet and turns to the speaker. "Hang on a minute. You're doing a great job. Some of us drank too much last night. *We* don't realize the importance of what *you're* saying about communicating with people who have different communication styles."

Then Lars begins calling names. "Paulette, you convinced our biggest client last year to bring three more states and their hospital systems to us. Let me ask you a question. Is your contact in the company more like you or different?" Paulette yells out, "So different! In fact, I didn't know how to communicate with her when we started. She's so data driven." Lars thanks her, then shouts out, "Jerry, you negotiated our lease three months ago and got one of the best agreements we ever had. How similar is the agent to you?" Jerry replies, "Extremely different." Lars turns to the group. "That's what I found too. If you want to survive at this company, you are going to do something different. Now, if any of you are fully satisfied with the requests you are making and your performance, feel free to leave and go take a nap. I'll be up front taking notes."

Master requesters appreciate insights, talents, and experiences that other people possess and they don't.

### Your Communication Bias
In the Ask Outrageously Study, respondents identified areas that affect how they make requests. Introversion was a problem often highlighted. Many mentioned:

- Family relationships and composition (birth order, single-parent household, relationship with parent)
- Upbringing and educational experiences (culture, religion, level of education)
- Work experiences (job responsibilities, leadership roles, mentors)
- Life experiences (health, marriage or divorce, political affiliation)

There are differences you may not be able to account for such as gender, generation, socioeconomic status, ethnicity, and religion. If you know little of a culture, check your assumptions with some questions. Perhaps someone is familiar with the person you are asking as well as the person's background and can give you some ideas on how to best communicate your request.

If you encounter difficulties communicating, explore the reasons those issues may exist. Perhaps it is your upbringing. Parenting approaches and family relationships were mentioned often by study participants. You may lack knowledge of or exposure to certain experiences or cultures. Reflecting on your reasons and whether they are well founded will help you in making requests and adapting your approach.

### Gender bias

In comments by respondents, gender was the most frequently mentioned factor shaping how people make requests. The comments were made only by women, and most sounded like this:

> *Girls in my family growing up were "support" people and were not expected to have a career or be on their own.*

> *I think women are expected to say thank you for whatever we're given, even if it's not what we wanted or less than we expected.*

> *I don't think women are taught that there are different rules for business. Being compensated or rewarded at work is not a gift. We've earned it.*

However, some women in the study said they were brought up to be strong or outspoken. They pointed to strong female role models in mothers, aunts, grandmothers, and supervisors as well as encouraging male role models, especially brothers, fathers, husbands, and bosses.

*I come from a long line of feisty women, feminine and strong.*

*I had three older brothers. My mom and dad told all of us we could do anything we wanted.*

*I give credit to the women's movement, and the Benedictine Sisters, who were models of asking outrageous questions to get what they needed to survive, build, and grow their hospitals and schools across the nation.*

The men surveyed made no comments that showed they felt an advantage or disadvantage in making requests because of their gender.

The Ask Outrageously Study agreed with previous research on asking. When men and women were surveyed, there were some variances but nothing significant (see Figure 9). The responses on two questions differed only slightly between men and women. Women reported a slightly higher preference, 6 percent, to make requests on behalf of others rather than themselves. However, both men and women felt much more comfortable when asking for another rather than for themselves.

On the second question the result was reversed (see Figure 10). Men were 6 percent more likely to have stopped themselves from asking for something big and then see the object of the request given to another.

### Why women don't ask

Other research has shown gender differences in requesting and negotiating.[1] In a study comparing male and female MBA students, male applicants were much more likely to negotiate their

---

1  Deborah A. Small, Michele Gelfand, Linda Babcock, and Hilary Gettman, "Who Goes to the Bargaining Table? The Influence of Gender and Framing on the Initiation of Negotiation," *Journal of Personality and Social Psychology* 93:4 (2007): 600–613.

job offers and request higher salaries than female applicants. Consequently, the women's average starting salaries were 8.5 percent lower than those of men. Not asking for more up front perpetuates over time and contributes to the overall gender salary gap. Linda Babcock and Sara Laschever, authors of *Women Don't Ask*, note the results:

> By neglecting to negotiate her starting salary for her first job, a woman may sacrifice over half a million dollars in earnings by the end of her career. Yet, as research reveals, men are four times more likely to ask for higher pay than are women with the same qualifications.

The stories of how to practically address the gender divide offer additional complexities for companies. Organizations attempt to be gender neutral in job descriptions and in creating salary ranges. Women's failure to ask puts human resources in a quandary. Human resources professionals wonder, "Do we offer

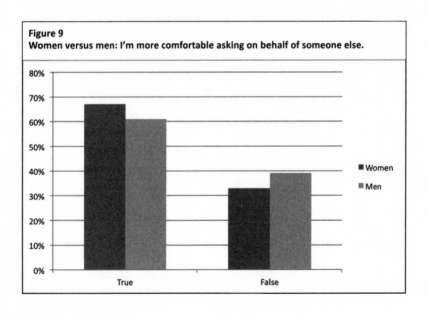

**Figure 9**
**Women versus men: I'm more comfortable asking on behalf of someone else.**

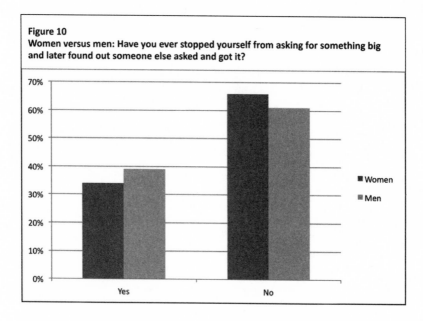

**Figure 10**
Women versus men: Have you ever stopped yourself from asking for something big and later found out someone else asked and got it?

more up front to women so we aren't perceived as discriminatory or is offering more itself a discriminatory practice?"

### What's the solution?

Marsha Clark, who has built a powerful reputation and network of influencers through her Power of Self program, suggests that the solution is "women supporting women." Marsha walks her talk by referring opportunities and making high-level connections. Research shows that women and men play a big role in encouraging women to ask. Giving responsibility, making introductions, and coaching goes a long way. Words of support to encourage women to speak up and ask include: "You can do this," and "No one is more capable or deserves this opportunity more."

*Howard*

Howard notices Sue's behavior in the board meeting and her failure to speak up. "What's up?" he asks. "I could tell you wanted to ask something, but it seemed like you were holding back." Sue confides that she doesn't feel comfortable yet with all the powerful leaders around the table. Howard responds, "Speak up and ask your questions. You were chosen to be here. Your voice needs to be heard. Whether you agree with them or me or not, what you say is important."

### Asking's biggest swear word

Prepare yourself for a frightening word: *Negotiation!* Women *and* men can be uncomfortable with the word "negotiation." It conjures up high-pressure sales or a need to defend against manipulation.

Negotiation apparently creates a fear of misrepresentation, being taken advantage of, tricks, and losing due to better preparation by the other side. Do you *really* worry you could lose your head or forget important details in the heat of the battle known as negotiation? You're strong, smart, and prepared. No one can mentally force *you* to submit to a position or overpower you with negotiation ninja moves. "Like it or not, you are a negotiator. Negotiation is a fact of life," say Roger Fisher and William L. Ury authors of the classic, *Getting to Yes: Negotiating Agreement Without Giving In.*

---

### Reality check: One word—"negotiation"— doesn't contain that type of power.

---

As Deborah Small and her research colleagues report in "Who Goes to the Bargaining Table?", negotiation is particularly intimidating to women. However, the gender differences *disappeared* when the same opportunities were framed as opportunities to ask. In other words, women perceive that asking is easier than negotiating.

Call the negotiation process "influencing" or "requesting" or "asking" instead. You *negotiate* when you *request* something (help, advice, money, better behavior) from someone else. In a negotiation, you make a series of requests. You ask questions to identify another's interests. They ask you about your interests. You exchange information. Together, you decide if the requests make sense and if you can agree. All the while, you attempt to build or strengthen a relationship.

Watch powerful negotiators in action. They ask questions, listen to answers, ask additional questions, and make the best decisions they can with the information they have. The best *negotiators* are the best *requesters*. They are respectful and at ease with everyone they meet from frontline staff to CEOs. And they ask questions all the time and everywhere.

### Language barriers

What happens when you don't speak the same language, literally? Language barriers make simple discussions difficult and complex conversations impossible. You miss subtleties and shortcuts to conversation. Often, common cultural phrases or references have different meanings. When basic language is an issue, more complicated communication such as making requests becomes nearly impossible. Don't give up.

While some instances call for an interpreter, most don't. When you deal with someone whose first language is different or who has a heavy accent, listen and repeat what you heard. They can correct you. Suggest that you two send emails detailing your different points. Then you can review and discuss the information, providing an opportunity to clarify the request. Also, a meeting in person or on video may be better than on the phone so you can read visual cues.

> *On conference calls with our partners in Mexico we ran into language issues. Our initial requests were in English. Our partners would discuss and debate the issue in Spanish, then give us the solution in English. They jokingly referred to their discussions as "Spanish Timeouts." While it took longer as we waited on the line, the end result was better communication, better understanding, and better answers to our questions.*

### Your accent or language

If you think your accent, jargon, or terminology is getting in the way of being heard and understood, ask for help. There are presentation coaches, speech therapists, and accent reduction experts who make their living helping others connect better. Help others understand you and your requests.

> *My role is to serve as a translator between the business needs and our software engineers. Not only is the jargon and information different, the way I communicate the messages to each group is different.*

### Stay positively curious

Include and connect with people who have different backgrounds. When you encourage participation and invite diverse voices to the conversation, you receive a deeper understanding of others' interests, an awareness of opportunities, and an enhanced ability to make more appropriate requests.

- Hang out where others hang out.
- Volunteer together.
- Make it a point to eat lunch with different people.

- Go to a festival or an exhibit featuring different cultures.
- Offer to mentor people with different backgrounds.
- Ask respectfully about a different practice.
- Listen, really listen, to what people are saying—and notice as well when they aren't saying anything.

### Sally

Sally and her husband Bryan chose to raise their family in a very diverse community. While they were active in their temple, most of her children's friends and their classmates weren't Jewish. Sally began hosting interfaith Passover dinners, called Seders. She asked their children's friends and families to attend, regardless of their religious beliefs. "Passover is a huge meal and there is so much tradition. It's cool for someone outside our faith to see it," Sally explains. "Growing up, I loved decorating a Christmas tree with my friend and hanging the lights. It's not just about religion. We're sharing our lives and different experiences."

Lenora Billings-Harris, author of *The Diversity Advantage,* explains, "We all see events through our own life experience lenses. The more we are willing to examine an opposing point of view, the more likely we are to withhold judgment until we have more facts."

No matter what, a willingness to learn and to ask questions will help you bridge cultural gaps. Make fewer statements of fact. You only know your own truth. Watch what others do that proves successful. Stay curious and ask respectful questions. Sandra Day O'Connor, the first female United States Supreme Court Justice, drew on her experiences as a rancher, a mother, and a volunteer to make this important point: "We don't accomplish anything in this world alone ... and whatever happens is the result of the whole tapestry of one's life and all the weavings of individual threads from one to another that creates something."

### Ask-sume instead of assume

Avoid assumptions based on appearance or background. The majority of people are honest, trustworthy, and well-intentioned. Remarkably, the people who help you the most often have very different upbringings and experiences. Steven M. R. Covey, author of *The Speed of Trust*, notes, "We judge ourselves by our intentions and others by their behavior."

 **Lead Others to Ask**

This Lead Others to Ask is intentionally longer. Bookmark this section. The areas covered offer you many of the largest opportunities to influence others to Ask Outrageously. Ask to meet regularly with each of your direct reports, people you coach, or people you influence. When meeting, be aware of people's tendencies or patterns when they communicate or ask. Review the DEAL strategy at the beginning of this chapter. Coaching others to make better, more frequent requests greatly depends on whether they like to Decide, Engage, Accommodate, or Leverage.

More reserved employees (Accommodators and Leveragers) might ask you important questions when you are alone. Schedule regular one-on-one meetings with them and let them know you'll be asking questions such as "What has worked this week?", "What would you like to improve the next week?", "How are you improving professionally?", or "What am I not asking you that might be helpful?" Scheduled meetings and expected questions require introverts to come to you with issues and suggestions.

Holding regularly scheduled one-on-one meetings with

extroverted employees (Deciders and Engagers) helps them be heard by their preferred audience, you. Your questions to them may be "What have you improved this week?" or "What's your focus and top three priorities for next week?" And if they approach you during the week, you could say, "Is this a priority right now, or can it wait until we meet during our one-on-one?" Scheduled meeting times can help extroverts reflect, focus, and prioritize.

Also, consider partnering extroverts and introverts together on projects and hold them accountable to report the outcomes of working together, especially in making requests. Let each know the other's strengths and ask them to support each other. Ask the introverts to help the extroverts in specific areas such as thinking through the details needed in requests or communicating in a way everyone understands. Have extroverts include introverts in meetings, presentations, and business networking opportunities. The real-life need to rely on and employ each other's strengths will drive their professional development far beyond any training or coaching.

In addition to DEAL styles and communication preferences, examine your leadership and team practices. Are there places people are excluded? Can you expose your team to more diversity and show the value of inclusion? Are you missing out on input and the wealth of diverse thinking? Are there people you can identify who need mentoring? Studies show your encouragement has an impact in boosting confidence and taking calculated risks. Meaningful words include, "I know you can do this," "What do you think? No one is more capable to represent us here," and "I wouldn't have given you the project, if I didn't think you were the perfect person to do it well."

Some inclusion practices are easy and fun. For instance, ask everyone on your team to bring in dishes or food from their culture or background for a large potluck luncheon. Make sure you bring in food that reflects your own background.

## Outrageous Review

- To know what works and what doesn't work when asking powerfully, assess the requesting style of others. Are they Deciders (serious and effective), Engagers (outgoing and relationship driven), Accommodators (pleasant and agreeable), or Leveragers (literal and fact driven)?
- We all have communication biases that reflect our upbringing, family relationships, and work/life experiences. Gender, ethnicity, religion, and socioeconomic status also influence how people ask and respond to requests.
- Gender was reported the most as a differentiator in making requests. Studies show that women don't make requests as frequently or easily as men in salary and interview negotiations.
- Although the percentages aren't significant, the Ask Outrageously Study showed that women are slightly more comfortable asking on behalf of someone else than men are. Men are slightly more likely to stop themselves from asking for something big and later finding out someone else asked for and got it.
- Both women and men become more anxious when the process is referred to as a "negotiation." Referring to the process as "influencing" or "requesting" reduces anxiety and eliminates the gender differences when asking.
- When you give yourself the gift of diverse experiences and a wealth of culture, you are able to connect more effectively and make inclusive requests.

**Smart Asks**

- How can I reframe a negotiation as a "request" or attempt to "influence"?
- When I make a request of someone, how does my DEAL style help me or hold me back?
- How would I make the same request to each of the DEAL types?

 **Ask List**

- See if you can determine which DEAL style people possess before making your request to them.
- Use your DEAL style to reach a goal.
- Identify your own communication biases. Take one action to stay curious, such as inviting someone new to lunch, visiting someone else's religious institution, or attending a cultural event.

 **Secret Success Tools**

Go to AskOutrageously.com and take the free assessments "What's Their DEAL?" and "What's My DEAL?" Share your results with a partner or work colleague.

# Eleven

# Calm under Pressure

Learning of a sudden change is unsettling. What happens when you discover all of your best-laid plans won't work? How do you refocus when you encounter unanticipated opposition? When you find you are unprepared, or everything you prepared isn't working, what do you do? Consider these situations.

- You arrive to discuss one matter with your boss and suddenly face an entirely different situation that negatively impacts your employment.
- Your client surprises you with bad news like dissatisfaction with your delivery schedule or budget cuts that will affect your project or your company.
- Your team member makes statements in a meeting that are different than you discussed, making you look uniformed.
- Your time to make a presentation is dramatically shortened.
- People ask questions you aren't prepared to answer.
- You broke a rule at work that you didn't know existed (such as acquiring equipment without going through proper channels or not following the procedure for requesting

time off). Your teammates are miffed, and there is a chill in the room when you enter.

## Buying Time

When an announcement comes as a shock, you may not have the time to contemplate your next request or response. Ask questions to seek clarity and help you decide your next-best step.

- "I'm not sure how to respond to that statement. If you were in my position, what would you be asking now?"
- "This information is new to me. Can you fill me in?"
- "That's surprising news. What are our options?"

Listen to the responses. Review the ASK Strategy (page 114) for tips on staying present and engaged under stressful situations.

### Sandy

Sandy's client sends her an email stating, "I just got your request for extending our contract. Are you kidding me? Your company can't live up to the services already promised. Doesn't your fulfillment team tell you what's going on?"

Though tempted to go directly to fulfillment and ask why she wasn't informed of an issue involving her biggest client, Sandy lets her client know she is concerned about preserving their relationship first. She responds to her client's email with a request: "I hate to hear this. I'm contacting fulfillment to investigate the issue immediately. If you have any relevant emails or information you can share, would you please send them to me? When can you talk this afternoon to discuss what progress was made?" Before Sandy makes the problem worse with promises she can't deliver, she will seek clarity from her fulfillment team.

When the unexpected occurs, stay creative and ask questions. Your plans may alter. You may not be excited about the change, but there are usually options.

Managing a rejection you didn't anticipate is difficult. It's especially tough when you find out you haven't followed a precedent or policy others think is *important*. Debating the system, arguing, begging, and walking away are bad strategies.

## Out of the Ordinary Requests

According to the Ask Outrageously Study, the number one reason people are likely to say no to a request is when the person is "asking for something inappropriate" (see page 23). When you make an unanticipated request, you may meet with resistance or an emotional response. Although your request seems logical, reasonable, and well thought out to you, it is new information to them. Take the time to slow down, communicate, and walk them through the basics. They may need time to reflect or ask for approval from their boss.

- Let people know you are aware that your request is different from the norm and a departure from standard process.
- Show you empathize with the challenges of their position or additional work the change may create.
- Give a few solid reasons to show the change an acceptable or allowable deviation. Make sure they see it isn't that big a departure from the norm.
- Ask what additional information they need to consider or communicate your request. If your message will be relayed to someone else on your behalf, provide written communication to properly support your request. You don't want to risk important asks on confusion or poor delivery.

Asking questions reveals areas of focus and areas to avoid. If you sense resistance, review the conversations or context in which they appeared. People give you clues to their thinking and actions in what they say. Most want a reason for a change or departure from the status quo. Your questions may not change their minds. However, responses to your questions provide insight and help you form options for your next attempt.

### *Ashton*

Corporate event planner Ashton is livid when she's told she can't use her usual audiovisual provider on her upcoming event. When Ashton investigates further, she is told, "Your AV company isn't on the preferred supplier list. Procurement created this process two months ago. Didn't you read the email?" Ashton chooses not to lose her temper about the change. She resists making unfruitful arguments about her experience in vetting quality AV providers. Instead, she asks, "How do we remedy this situation? This is the best AV provider for our events and critical to the success of our future conferences." Ashton is told if she "fills out the paperwork and the AV providers show proof of the new insurance required, the company can be added back to the provider list."

One of the most exasperating situations is when you have an emergency or need an immediate solution to a problem. Have you ever been placed on hold or told to follow a process that you know won't work?

If there is no process for emergencies or exceptions, use these questions.

- "What would you recommend?"
- "If you were in my situation and you had to get an answer immediately, what would you do?"
- "Is there anything I can do to help make this request easier on you?"

### Melissa

Melissa approaches sourcing for additional contractors to complete a prominent project on time. She just learned of the need, so she couldn't submit her request through the online tool and now she risks a delay of up to three weeks. "I understand the need for rules and procedures, especially when requesting resources. Unfortunately, this is a critical request that impacts both the client's services and revenue. The need for additional people was just identified." She asks, "What is the procedure in emergency situations like this?"

## Control in Critical Situations

Take control of critical or highly stressful situations through questions. Police, medical professionals, and firefighters ask questions: "Are you hurt?" "Did you see what happened?" "Are there others in the building?" "What can you tell me?" When you are communicating with someone facing a stressful situation, ask questions to provide you the information you need. Answering questions can be calming because responding helps people think and focus their communication.

### Brooke

Brooke can tell her client is nervous about visiting her financial planning office. She asks her client for permission to take control of their conversation: "Micha, I want to make the most of our time together. If it is agreeable to you, I'll ask you several questions about your estate and retirement planning over the next hour. If I hear enough of an explanation or if I am unclear about your answer, may I have your permission to interrupt you?" Brooke's questions redirect Micha's focus. He nods and looks relieved.

### Asking for information from the reluctant

Obtaining an estimate or "guesstimate" of any kind can be difficult because people don't want to mislead or disappoint you by providing information before they can investigate. Sometimes you need to make decisions on the limited information available at the time. Other times you need to gauge the severity or frequency of an issue. When people are vague or refuse to give you a direct answer or even an idea, how do you nail them down with specifics? *You don't*. Instead, ask for a range or average.

Gather the best information you can by posing these less-intimidating questions.

- "I understand the real answer will depend on your findings. Knowing just what you know now, what do you think we should be considering?"
- "Just so I can get a grasp on this situation, what are usually the best-case and worst-case scenarios?"
- "You've done this job for years. How often does this type of situation occur?"

### Amelia

Amelia is waiting to find out if her computer repair is a simple fix or a more extensive one. The technical support professional is reluctant to give her an estimated time frame. He tells her, "I'm not sure what's wrong until I get into the system to figure it out." Amelia asks, "Approximately how long does it take you to examine an operating system to determine what's wrong?" She adds a reason she needs to know, "I am trying to decide if I need to reschedule a meeting. Best-case and worst-case, how long could it take?"

### Dante

An engineer and leader in charge of maintaining consistent client services for a large cellular phone company, Dante needs to determine how his client might be impacted when it makes a big change to its service. Dante wants to prep his client and have the appropriate staff on call. However, his installers won't give him any answers on the severity of the potential risk or the possible duration. Dante tells his lead installer, "I am not holding you to the specifics. I simply need to get an idea of the potential regions this could affect and the possible time involved. In the past year, you've done 150 of these installations. How many of those experienced service issues for two hours or more?"

### When you are reluctant

People are welcome to ask openly. You also have a right *not* to answer. Answering some questions may reveal confidential information, give away trade secrets, or disclose information you don't want known. Sometimes the requests sound more like demands or even threats. How do you respond to a question when the answer is something you don't want to share? If you don't want to respond, go to a question.

- "I'm not privy to that information. What are you hoping to determine?"

- "Which particular area or item do you have a question about?"
- "Can you tell me what you're seeking?"

### Zan

Zan is the account manager for an elevator company. Her customer asks her to "break down each and every one of your costs in this proposal." Responding to the request would reveal confidential company information and trade secrets. Instead, Zan smiles and says, "I'm not going to tell you. You know I can't break this down into line items. What do you really need to know to determine if our proposal is a fit?"

You don't have to answer, and you can say no to people who attempt to take advantage of you. Let people know your limits and when their requests aren't appropriate.

---

**They can ask but you don't have to tell.**

---

### Donna

Donna is the owner of a promotional products company. She has invested hours selecting appropriate items that complement her client's brand to distribute at his annual tradeshow. She asked manufacturers for favors to expedite the order and reduce the price. Before Donna places the order, her client calls her with a final request. "Donna, can you cut our order in half? Just delete the pens and send us the artwork you created. We've found a pen five cents cheaper online."

Donna handles this latest request adeptly: "No, I can't. The way I get paid for my thought process and professional services is through the products you order through me. I've negotiated a great price for you and asked for favors from manufacturers I trust. Are you ready to place the entire order through my company or do you want to start the process with someone new?"

### Sensitive questions

Speaking of boundaries, have you ever had someone ask a personal question about a decision you made? These questions usually start with a "Why did you _____?" For example, "Why did you: Change professions? Go back to school? Take a break in your employment? Become a parent? Get that tattoo? Choose to vote the way you did?"

You'd be justified to say, "Mind your own business." However, you can refuse to respond *and* maintain the relationship, even when someone is only seeking to be "right" or debate your choices. Give a quick, noncommittal response then redirect the conversation with a question. Try these responses:

- "Wow. Answering that question would take more time than either of us has. Are you ready to get started on this new project?"
- "Sounds like you've made a decision that works for you. Are you ready to tackle what's next on this to do list?"
- "There is probably nothing I have to add that you haven't already heard or thought through. Should we get back to what we were doing?"

Approachability and honest communication are keys to getting what you really want. However, you can choose what information is appropriate to share with others. And you can be selective as to who and what receives your time and resources.

## Be Selective with Your Yes

Former Governor of Texas Ann Richards once told a small group of young women leaders in the first Power Pipeline class to limit donations and involvement to a few organizations. "Say 'no' unless you can make a difference," she advised. "You dilute your power and funds by saying 'yes' to everyone. Instead of giving a trivial amount to many, give more funds to a few you believe in. You'll be surprised at how little money it takes to be recognized as a leader and make a difference."

### Asking the opinionated

Have you ever made requests to people who refused to consider others' views? They aren't open to any opinions but their own. Often, they are strong supporters of political candidates, a religion, or a particular sports team. They listen so they can tell you the reasons you are wrong and convince you they are right.

At work, when you ask these opinionated people to change their mindset, they say, "We've never done it that way." "We don't need to fix something that isn't broken." "When we tried something different in the past, it didn't work." These skeptics and naysayers are adamant they are correct and any change will bring failure. It is either their way or the highway.

How do you ask them to try something different when their tendency is to follow established ways? You ask if they are *willing to explore* or *to consider* a possibility first.

- *"If* there were options that would get you better results, would you be open to *exploring* those options or upgrades?"
- *"If* it were possible to continue the same high level of service or improve it, would you be *willing to consider* other ways of operating?"

When people promise to explore or consider, they create an agreement with you. Later, if they claim "that way would never work" or "no smart person would do that," remind them of their agreement. "Hang on; you agreed to consider the options. We aren't changing anything now. We agreed to simply explore how an upgrade might work."

If you ask people to explore possibilities and they say no, seek clarification. "You aren't willing to explore or consider any better ways, correct?" Some will agree and others won't. Stop asking when you hear people protect their position or perceived control. For instance, "You couldn't tell me anything that would change my mind. I'm not going to break something that already works."

You are wasting your time trying to convince someone who is not willing to change. You are done. Say OK and move on. If he or she later asks, "So what is your idea? What did you want to talk about?" your response is, "You've told me you aren't interested in exploring possible improvements. I respect your decision."

### Ask Away or Walk Away

How do you determine whether you should continue dealing with someone or are wasting your time? First you decide if your requests are being heard. If so, keep at it and ask away. If you are wasting your time, you walk or run away.

### *Ask away*

You are moving in a positive direction. Continue to ask when people:

- Ask you to explain how you arrived at your conclusions or your thinking.
- Exhibit body language that shows they are listening, taking in your points, and considering your request.

- Disagree with you but are not disagreeable.
- Discuss information in a rational and respectful manner.
- Educate you on something new or provide information and insight.
- Are not agreeing but continue to listen and participate in the conversation.
- Knowingly or unknowingly are teaching you about the process or players involved.
- Agrees that they want to work with you but are just not sure how yet.

---

**When you get to an objection, don't start selling, start asking.**

---

### Walk away

When interactions are unproductive and heading nowhere, it's time to leave. Walk away when a person:

- Clearly has no power or authority to say yes or even influence a yes.
- Begins acting obnoxiously or is rude or disrespectful.
- Is opinionated and/or resistant to any change and shuts you down completely.
- Begins packing up to leave and/or says, "I have no more time for this."
- Lies to you. *If* you decide to stay, you must proceed with great caution. Require outside confirmation of any promises or assertions.
- Sets you up to look bad or make a mistake.
- Is on a fishing expedition, looking for information but not sharing in exchange.

- Creates roadblocks with nowhere for you to go.

Say "It's time for a break" or "Let's postpone and talk later." Then excuse yourself.

You know the difference between a self-limiting belief and a risk to your well-being. If you think you might be in real danger or you see an alarming change in someone's demeanor, say "Look at the time. I'm sorry. I've got to go." If your gut tells you there is danger, don't ignore the feeling. Leave.

## Cool, Calm, and in Control

The saying "never let them see you sweat" is appropriate. Once you become angry or frustrated instead of in control and logical, you face coming out on the losing end of the agreement. Instead, take a break. If you need help managing the emotions you encounter, remember the ASK Strategy (see page 114).

It's hard to find the right words when you're emotionally compromised. Remain cool, calm, and in control despite others' reactions, negative behavior, or responses including an emphatic no. You may need to help them seek clarity as well. Use your "what" and "how" questions. Sometimes you need to regroup and seek further clarification before asking.

### When you're let down by others

When you ask for help, it is disappointing when people ignore or deny your request. However, few things are more exasperating than when others don't honor their commitments or perform the jobs they are hired to do. People you rely on can let you down.

#### Danny

It is 7:45 a.m. The meeting starts at 8:00 a.m. Danny is the only one there from his team. His peers promised they would show up early to help set up the room but didn't. One has a sick daughter, another overslept, and one team member is stuck in traffic.

If the people you ask have a history of overpromising and underdelivering, create a backup plan. Assume the worst and prepare for it. Safeguard your word, reputation, and results. Then hope for the best, and if it happens, celebrate. You can't change that some won't do their job or live up to their promises. However, you can change your requests and your responses.

### Janet

Janet can't get her coworker Paul to provide timely reports on a critical project. Instead he provides excuses, and he tells her to "get in line behind all the others." Janet replies, "Paul, the system designers and I need your reports by 1:00 tomorrow afternoon for our 2:00 p.m. call. On the call, I will confirm that you and I discussed the importance of providing these updated reports each week. Can I say you've committed to send the reports each Tuesday?" Janet asks and gives Paul a choice. Whether Paul says yes or no, Janet can announce his decision to the team. The team can decide the next steps if the answer is no. If Paul agrees to provide the reports and doesn't deliver as promised, he is breaking his commitment and letting the team down.

### Robin

Because of her superior customer service, Robin was recently promoted to manager. However, she can't get her employees to serve customers with the same enthusiasm. They won't honor her requests, and work isn't getting done. Begging, pleading, and threatening aren't working. Robin is the boss and in a position of authority. She decides to inform her employees of their job duties and ask if they agree to assume their responsibilities. If employees decide not to perform the job they are paid to do, Robin can ask them to leave.

Some would argue this is more of a Robin problem than a managerial problem. Often when an employee is promoted to influence people who were once peers, the new manager lacks leadership training in coaching, counseling, and communication skills. The most powerful skills that leaders can learn are how to make requests, gain commitments, and follow through.

The need for improvement is most obvious in performance management and disciplinary skills. Dick Grote, author of *Discipline without Punishment,* offers this advice: "Have courage. People who won't comply with your requests may need to find another place to work, one where the standards are low enough for them to be successful."

Life and work are full of surprises, and not all are pleasant. When the negative news involves your employment, it can feel like a personal attack. Have you ever tried to remain positive when the conversation involves discipline, poor performance, layoffs, or termination? Review the ASK Strategy if you think you may be facing one of these tough discussions in your future.

If you've never experienced a difficult conversation, what do you think is the reason? Is it your superior performance? Has your leadership failed to give you candid feedback? Or, are you playing things too safe by not requesting more responsibility or taking calculated risks?

### Have you been excluded?

Making powerful requests is nearly impossible when you miss important conversations, policy making, and/or key decisions. Whether the exclusion is intentional or not, you are being left out of valuable information and insights. You can't play the game if you don't know the rules or where the game is being held.

Even though you've made sure there are no communication or technical glitches, you continue to be effectively locked out of the decision-making process. There are signs you are being excluded. Despite your best efforts to reach out, you are:

- Ignored when requesting to be included in events, calls, or meetings.
- Diverted or left out of informal conversations or functions.
- Left off important correspondence and email chains.
- Not provided the new standards or changes to processes or resources.
- Not invited to the meeting or the separate meeting before the meeting.

Do you ever feel that people shut you out of the conversation? Sometimes the exclusion occurs through their lack of responses to your requests or failure to invite you to conversations. At times you can be present when the conversation occurs but be ignored, interrupted, or talked over. Meetings can be the worst because the more verbally confident can direct and divert the conversations away from your requests and input.

### Fran

Fran has a serious concern about proceeding with the proposed investors without checking into their portfolio. When she raises her doubts to the selection team, she is told, "Fran, we want to make this deal work. No one else is worried that something is wrong."

Fran thinks she is making a reasonable request, so she speaks up again. "We need to look at this carefully. Each of us has a fiduciary duty, and we don't want to subject ourselves to risk. How can we get a better look at the financials before entering into the venture?" Her mention of liability gains attention. Fran gets the investors' financials and finds her suspicions are correct.

### Win the games people play

To get around exclusions and determine hidden agendas, make alliances one at a time with people who are in the loop. If there is a meeting notice you don't receive, see if an assistant or someone else will copy you. Watch for patterns such as meeting days and times. Talk one-on-one and ask clarifying questions.

People who discount you are underestimating your abilities. Use it to your advantage. When you ask outrageously, they may let their guard down and give you more information or a better result. Someone may not understand your expertise or the experience you bring to the table. That's OK. Too much people-pleasing behavior can hinder your success.

*People can think I'm as naive as they want, as long as I get what I want.*

*He thinks I'm stupid, because I'm shorter and look young. I'm not complaining. His mistake worked to my advantage. He didn't even counter my request. I would have taken much less.*

### Uninstall Your "Like Me" Button

Know what is difficult? Some people won't be happy with your requests. Not everyone will like you or approve of your asking. Honestly, these aren't bad things. You don't need approval from everyone, especially strangers or people you rarely see. Some random person's judgment is not going to pay your bills. You won't change that person. Mentally wish this person the best and move on to a more receptive audience.

Karen Anne Byars Hall, sales expert, provided a tough-love response to her sister about reasons others aren't being inclusive:

> If people don't like you, [probably] nothing you do is going to change their minds. Do you readily change your opinion of others? Sorry. There is nothing you can do about it, so let it go. However, the good news is with the people who like you. It's hard for them to change their minds as well.

When you encounter people who are judgmental, condescending, negative, or toxic, it helps to remember not to adopt their thinking. They have their own issues and problems. Do not allow those people to rent space in your head. Evict them.

---

*Never wrestle with a pig. You both get dirty but only the pig likes it.* — **Texas saying**

---

### Toxic People

Ever sense you are experiencing a grown-up version of junior high? The same mean kids can grow into mean adults intent on making others miserable. In the extreme, you may be dealing with a narcissist or someone with no conscience. You will not win over the narcissistic manipulators.

Stay professional and emotionally detached with your requests and responses. Do not reveal personal information or vulnerabilities which give them a better advantage to snub you or stab you in the back. Protect yourself by asking for clarification on any projects or communication. Then, document responses. Use stealth. Ask for help from a counselor, executive coach, mentor, and/or human resources.

High-pressure tactics aren't effective in building long-term relationships. Realistically, no one can force someone to take a deal and expect another party to willingly adhere to the agreement. Instead of asking and creating a durable relationship, the party who feels intimidated often looks for opportunities to sabotage the deal.

It's OK to call the other side's bluff when they say no or give you a senseless response. You may also choose to tolerate their behavior if it doesn't hurt you. You don't need to point out their "tell" if you don't want. (Besides, they may change their strategy if you do.) Double-check the other person's assertions. And question any responses that don't sound right. Remain focused on your goals and stand your ground. You are in much better shape standing your ground than trying a counterattack.

### Don't make an obnoxious ask of yourself

Avoid ultimatums and don't use tricks when asking. You are prepared. Resist the urge to get drawn into amateurish tactics that are structured to throw people off emotionally such as yelling, flinching, sighing, or eye rolling. Once you spot others using them, they lose credibility.

Ask big to start and then refrain from nitpicking over minutiae. If you "nibble" too much, you eventually "bite" or irritate the people you are asking, and they will walk away. Be able to support any request you make. You don't need unprofessional or sneaky schemes. They rarely work, especially for high-stakes request. Stay respectful, even if other people aren't. Their bad behavior may come back to haunt them.

### Adjust your ask

Don't become so fixated and dedicated to one path that you can't take another. As long as you reach your destination, the route

---

### Asking Tricks and Tactics

Common tricks and tactics designed to throw people off emotionally include:

- Flinching, sighing, or eye rolling to make you feel uneasy or question your request.
- Pretending they suddenly need to check with a higher authority.
- Playing good cop/bad cop: "I'm the good guy. The other person is a bad guy and not as generous."
- Attempting to get you to bid against yourself or gain more after a request is granted or an agreement made.

For a more complete list of Asking Tricks and Tactics you may encounter as well as the counter requests, go to AskOutrageously.com

---

you take doesn't have to be precisely the one you planned. Be flexible and leave yourself open to possibilities. When you make a mistake, fix what you can and adjust your course.

 **Lead Others to Ask**

Ask people you lead to describe how they will improve their performance. Let them know the standards you expect. Respectfully treat others as adults fully capable of deciding their future.

Ask a poorly performing employee to *choose* between improving performance and leaving to find another employment opportunity. Stop being the rules enforcer. Exiting is an especially powerful mandate with a huge potential payoff. Your request has beneficial ramifications on coworkers who closely watch to see if your asks are serious or not.

### Outrageous Review

- Just because you have information doesn't mean you have to reveal it.
- When you are faced with an unpleasant surprise or an unexpected response, remain calm and go to a question.
- Don't make an obnoxious ask out of yourself. Avoid ultimatums when asking. Preparation beats any trick or tactic.
- When making a request, be comfortable when you hear silence. Allow the person you are asking to formulate a response. Resist the urge to fill the silence with nervous chatter.

 ### Smart Asks

- What approaches have worked for me in the past when making requests?
- When did I receive a pleasant surprise beyond what I thought possible?
- How will I respond if I don't get the response I want or was expecting?
- That's weird behavior. Are they trying a tactic on me?
- If someone I care about wanted to make the same request, what would I tell them to do?

 ### Ask List

Start looking for the three common asking tactics. Practice using counter-requests. Stay calm and focused.

- **Set Aside Tactic.** Ask to stay on the current topic when others try the tactic of changing the subject. Be ready when people say, "Let's set that aside for now and talk about these other issues." Counter-request the Set Aside tactic by saying, "No, this is the main issue for me. I want us to resolve it first."

- **Higher Authority Tactic.** Ask the person about the criteria used to make a decision and ask for support or proof. When others say they need to get approval from their boss, committee, or board of directors, counter-request the Higher Authority tactic by saying, "They usually follow your recommendations, don't they?" or "You are recommending what I'm asking, correct?"
- **Low-Ball or High-Ball Tactic.** They make an unfounded or ridiculous request at the start. Ask others how they reached their conclusion when you hear a request that doesn't make sense. Stay calm and counter-request, "Can you walk me through your thinking?" or "Can you show me how you came to these numbers?" What may look like a ridiculous request may be a miscommunication. Either they need to be educated or you do.

 ## Secret Success Tools

For a list of "Asking Tricks and Tactics" people may use and counter-requests you can use to respond, go to AskOutrageously.com.

# Twelve

# Outrageous Results

When you ask outrageously, your results become bigger as well. The stakes are higher, there are more people involved, and there are more moving parts. While some shy away from managing high-stakes deals, managing many little opportunities can be more difficult and not as rewarding. There's a saying in the South, "It ain't bragging if you've done it." The strategies and wisdom in this section come from those who have "done it," people who made successful requests when the stakes were high. Review the best practices of those who regularly ask outrageously. Decide which strategies will work to upgrade your asking results.

## High-Stakes Requests

High-stakes requests often involve high dollar figures. Continuing to playing it safe will get you more of what you already have. To achieve outstanding outcomes, you have to ask differently and/or for something different.

*Although I received approval from my boss and her supervisor to write off about $2 million in debt, I asked outrageously. I made one last call to the dealership and asked them to pay us, an auto-*

*mobile holding company, what they owed. They wired the money that night.*

When you approach bigger or high-stakes requests, the preparation is usually more involved. You consider more stakeholders' positions and strategize around additional interests, issues, and objectives. The increased scrutiny and multiple interests don't need to overwhelm you.

In some ways, high-stakes requests are easier than simpler ones because people are more focused on the larger outcome instead of the smaller pieces. Interestingly, people's personal attachment to outcomes in high-stakes requests can decrease. For instance, $10,000 can affect a small business's bottom line. However, if the request involves a million dollars, a $10,000 variance is not a large concern.

### Break down the request

Master requesters view more complicated high-stakes opportunities as a *series* of requests made over time to different people. Often high-stakes opportunities require patience mixed with diligence and attention to specifics. Detailed requests, like technical proposals, have strong tools in place to keep track of the back-and-forth. Concentrate on breaking down big requests into smaller ones.

### Byron

As a senior engineer for a large defense contractor, Byron's role was proposing modifications to existing aircraft owned by the military and NASA. Remarkably, Byron had a perfect record with these high-stakes proposals. If the government decided to proceed with the project, it awarded the contract to Byron's company. What was Byron's secret to landing multiple contracts worth millions of dollars? "I read the scope of their RFP and gave them exactly what they requested. I answered every question they asked. No matter their request, I showed line by line where they could find the solution. When we asked them to consider our solution, I was very clear and used plain English where possible instead of unnecessary technical terms. And, if we offered a different solution than what was asked, I put that option in a separate proposal."

### Focus on value

Making high-stakes requests requires confidence and a little bit of chutzpah. Requests made for high-stakes compensation or positions often revolve around the value you bring to your organization. The importance of showing your contribution is key. Driving results and achieving unprecedented outcomes demand attention. Compensation, benefits, and often ownership is paid to keep high performers to continue their input. Your contribution may be valued more than you perceive.

> *I asked for and received the majority ownership in a business I grew but didn't start. My request was not traditional and the founder pushed back. However, the board agreed my contribution and leadership merited the increased ownership interest.*

> *Instead of simply quitting my executive-level position, I asked for a six-figure severance package to transition to the next leader—and got it!*

Dianna Booher, communication expert and author of *Communicate Like a Leader*, reminds us, "Humility and self-confidence are not mutually exclusive qualities. You need both humility and self-confidence to have the right estimate of yourself."

## Challenge the norms

Master requesters challenge the norms and don't do business as usual. Master requesters are leaders of people and approaches. That means they are asking and thinking more creatively than most can do. The outcomes, and even the attempts, are noticed by even higher-level decision makers, a.k.a. the only ones that matter. Are you willing to push back or disrupt thinking? You may have to ruffle some feathers.

> *We asked our clients to buy a different version of our product, which went against industry norms. Our customers were asked to pay the same cost, though it cost us substantially less. Some clients didn't like the change, but most loved it. The new offering also added millions to our bottom line.*

### Sui

As an executive recruiter for a global search firm in New York, Sui asked questions that seemed obvious to her. Sui's responsibilities were to place C-Suite executives (CEO, CMO, CFO, CTO, etc.) in major companies with the fee ranging between $300,000 to $1 million for filling one position. She risked the substantial fee and surprised one client by asking, "What's wrong with the job? Or better yet, what's wrong with the organization? Why don't you have viable candidates and a good onboarding system?" She questioned the high turnover and the lack of homegrown talent. "What was probably outrageous to the recipient was my audacity or confidence to ask such a question. And more importantly … I put them on the spot to answer!" Sui won the client's respect and future business by fighting the "anxiousness to close the deal, get the job, or take the money and run."

Are you prepared to ask for forgiveness after the fact? Not everyone will be comfortable with your change in approach or going outside the norm.

### David

A managing partner in a car dealership, David Thomas was faced with high inventory and slow sales. While prospecting for fleet sales, he called a large national car rental brand and pitched a fifty-car sale. After a brief visit, the car rental company increased that number and placed the order of a lifetime for 2,000 cars, a $40 million order! Very excited, David called his factory dealer representative to request and submit a sale order to trigger the manufacture of 2,000 cars.

Instead of congratulations, David received a less-than-favorable response from the factory representative: "No dealer has had a 2,000-unit order and the fleet customer should just contact the factory direct." Repeated conversations went nowhere, so David made another high-stakes request and boldly called the CEO of the brand to request the order be placed immediately.

On a call the next day with the CEO, the national sales VP, and the manufacturing VP, the CEO asked David why the national car rental company was dealing directly with him and not the factory fleet department that traditionally handles large orders. David responded, "I asked the same thing from my prospect. He told me, 'The factory rep would never return my calls. I want to buy cars, a lot of cars. You called me and offered cars for sale. I need them. I'll take them.'" "Look," David told the group, "It's my job as a car dealer to sell cars. I don't say no to doing more business." The CEO agreed.

David made the $40 million sale, then made a *second* sale for $40 million, *and* was paid the compensation for both. He is now part-owner of a large auto group. "We will sell 15,000 cars this year. I prospect and ask for business daily."

### High-stakes advice

How would you advise someone you cared about to improve his or her outcomes? When asked, survey respondents suggested practicing with roleplays and providing stories. Overwhelmingly their advice is to take the risk and just ask.

*Feel the fear and ask anyway.*

*You don't get what you don't ask for.*

*What's the worst that can happen?*

## Permission to Ask

You have addressed your fears and blocks. You tried all the breakthrough strategies. Yet, you still aren't asking for what you really want. What's up? Could you be waiting to ask outrageously until your requests are "blessed" or approved?

Are you waiting for permission? Answer these questions:

- Do you survey your friends or seek consensus from your peers first?
- Are you researching to find the perfect article, book, or website with information that gives you the confidence to proceed?
- Do you mentally run through multiple scenarios or a pros-and-cons list—and never take action?
- Are you waiting for someone to grant you permission?

Although having a friend agree with you is reassuring, do you really need a friend's approval? Your system of researching or polling opinions seems like a lot of work! Are you looking for an authority figure or expert to grant you permission? No problem. Look no further. Your permission to ask is *granted*.

---

**You are hereby granted full permission to ask outrageously. You are permitted to tap into whatever resources, efforts, and talents you deem necessary to get what you *really* want.**

---

Do you know what you want? If so, grant yourself permission to ask without all the advance work. Allow yourself to succeed. Then call your friend and celebrate.

### Best Practices of Master Requesters

The strategies of those who ask outrageously often build on one another. These best practices work in high-stakes requests and to powerfully influence others.

**Go face-to-face.** It's easier to tell someone no by email or text. If at all possible, go face-to-face and persuade on a personal level. Communication via technology eliminates many rapport-building opportunities. Find ways to talk to human beings instead of pressing buttons and filling in forms. Invent ways for others to put a face to your voice or a voice to your email message.

*I am a very good listener, and I read people's body language. I try to avoid lengthy conversations on the phone or through email.*

**Plan for the worst and hope for the best.** Prepare for plans to go awry. Don't be thrown when a person takes a different stance than expected.

**Be flexible when making a request.** Remain focused on the outcome and let go of the exact strategy for achieving your result. Concentrate on areas you can control.

**Question others' answers.** Don't believe everything you are told. Not everything you hear is accurate. Trust your instincts. If what you are told "smells funny," is illogical, or departs from previous information that you were provided, ask for independent support or verification.

---

### Figures can lie and liars can figure.

---

**Know your facts.** When someone appears to be more influential or powerful, beef up your preparation. Know your numbers. Ask about the method used to arrive at the estimation. Question the value reported. Mistakes are made.

**Stay in the question.** The more the other side talks, the better your deal. Ask for explanations. Question how they came to their conclusions. Determine the other side's motivations and true interests through questions. Ask, ask, ask.

**Learn from the mistakes of others.** Ask others what worked or didn't work for them *before* making your request. Find someone else who has been successful and follow his or her model. You don't have time to make all the mistakes.

**Have a sense of humor.** Don't have a sense of humor? Go find one. Your attitude and sanity need you to lighten up. Instead of blowing up, find humor in absurd requests.

> *I would always bring one of my customers his favorite Starbucks drink when I was asking for a favor. It became a joke. When he saw me coming with coffee, he'd automatically say, "What do you want now?" Even if I was nervous about asking, the mood was lightened.*

**Make the best request for now.** Many bargains are struck with facts available at that time. The same scenario, stakeholders, and limitations may never be present again. Ask yourself, "Is this the best request I can achieve right now, with the people present and the information I know?"

**Weigh the response.** Your request may result in conflicting recommendations and unsolicited advice. Consider suggestions offered and the source. Then weigh the advice to determine what best suits you and your situation.

**Give yourself a break.** Stop worrying about leaving something on the table or missing out on a better deal. Prepare as well as you can under the circumstances and ask. It's true that with more time or more information, you *might* reach a better outcome. However, more time and delays might cause a deal to fall apart. Also, the other party might go elsewhere or find information to use against you.

**Honor your agreements.** To the best of your abilities do what you say you will.

**Maintain relationships.** Do not flaunt a power imbalance. You never know when the power may shift and leave you in a weaker position. Whether your request is granted or not, leave on good terms. You may see the same players again.

**Don't become too attached to your requests.** Avoid becoming so entrenched in the process that you agree to take undesired options. Rarely is there only one choice.

**Be willing to walk away.** Once you lose your ability to walk away from a deal, you greatly decrease your power in any request. Always leave yourself an out and know your options if the current request does not work out.

**Put agreements in writing.** A solid practice to ensure clear communication in even small agreements is to confirm your understanding in writing. People's memories fade. Clear up any misunderstandings before they become deal breakers. If your request is accepted, at least send a follow-up note or email.

**Be realistic.** When you review your efforts, be kind to yourself. Consider the possibilities available, the timeline you faced, and the result you achieved. Not every request happens the way you anticipate. Not every request should be or will be granted.

**Ask outrageously.** No, it isn't greedy to ask for more. You never know when you might get a little extra. If you don't ask for more, you have nothing to barter with to get something reasonable. Make outrageous requests. See what happens.

If you've gotten this far and asked these outrageous asks, you've earned a Masters in Requests. Congrats!!!

 **Lead Others to Ask**

- Ask those you lead and those you coach to watch a great negotiator or dealmaker in addition to yourself. Have them debrief which of the best practices they observe.
- Ask people to identify two high-stakes opportunities and go for them. Let them know they can come to you for guidance.

**Outrageous Review**

- High-stakes requests have more moving parts. Stay organized. In some ways, they are easier because people are more focused on the larger outcome and not as personally attached to the smaller pieces or dollar amounts.
- The best requesters have a sense of humor, know the facts, and are realistic. Be satisfied with a deal you have made.

Don't second-guess how it played out or worry that you've left money on the table or that terms could have been better. If you are satisfied with the deal when it was made, move on.

- Live in the question. The more someone else talks, the better. Determine the others' motivations and true interests through questions. Ask, ask, ask.
- Be able to answer the question, "Is this the best request I can achieve right now, with the people present and the information I know?" Although more time and information *might* enhance your results, delays give the other side time for additional insight or more information too.
- Be willing to walk away. Once you lose your ability to walk away from a deal, you lose your power. Always leave yourself an out and know your options if the current request does not work out.

### Smart Asks

- If I'm told no, what is my Plan B?
- Don't stall. What is the best request I can make right now with the information I have?
- How can I watch a Master Requester in action?

### Ask List

- Ask in person. Instead of emailing a question to your boss or coworker, pick up the phone or, if possible, walk over to someone's desk and ask face-to-face.
- Ask with documentation. At least follow up a successful request with an email outlining the agreement reached by the parties. (You'll thank yourself later.)
- Watch Master Requesters in action. See which practices they use.

**Secret Success Tools**

Go to AskOutrageously.com to print off an Official Permission Slip to Ask. If you've read to this point and done the activities, you've earned a Masters in Request. You are a "smart ask" who is achieving Outstanding Results.

Congratulations! Go to AskOutrageously.com and download your Official Masters in Request certificate.

# A Final Note

Outrageous asking works. Over and over again, experience and research show that people achieve far greater outcomes than they believed possible. They ask questions that change their lives and the lives of others. And they get outrageous outcomes.

Writing this book forced me to walk my talk and ask outrageously. From the initial book proposal to the final manuscript submission, I ventured outside my comfort zone and asked for what I really wanted. Despite my overanalyzing and concern regarding each request, the responses and results have been overwhelmingly positive and affirming.

On this project, I've experienced outstanding outcomes and developed valuable relationships by asking outrageously. My friends have helped with my book proposal, introduced me to a publisher, provided in-depth editing, and suggested revisions. When asked, my speaking and business friends assisted me in more than doubling my research responses in less than a week. People I deeply respect were delighted to give quotes and endorsements. In asking for help to get ready for the TEDx-SMU talk that evolved into this book, my friends coached, encouraged, and even prodded me to be better.

Success goes to those who are willing to ask. Ask often. And ask outrageously.

Did writing this book help me overcome my regrets over failing to ask Jay Leno for a picture all those years ago? *Great question!* Actually *applying* the lessons improved my outlook and outcome. The *week* the draft of this book was due to the publisher, Jay came to *my* hometown of Dallas to perform. We sent a few emails to Jay's representatives and launched a quick social media campaign to ask for his picture. (Apparently, we were a little overzealous in our attempts. Jay's office helpfully informed us that there is a fine line between *asking outrageously* and *stalking*.)

*Guess what? Asking outrageously worked again!*

We received backstage passes. My husband, friends, and I got to meet Jay Leno before his show. Jay was gracious. Later, we watched Jay in his element. He commanded the stage, kept the audience laughing for an hour and a half, *and* I got my picture!

Which brings us to our last lesson:

*When you get what you want … stop and celebrate!*

At the end of this book, the advice is still the same. Concentrate on what you are seeking and connect with the people who can help you achieve it. You can do this. Breakthroughs and outrageous outcomes are waiting for you.

You need to ask to know. You need to ask to grow. (And sometimes you need to ask to meet Jay Leno.) *Now, go be a smart ask and ask outrageously!*

# Resources

## Secret Success Tools Available at AskOutrageously.com

The tools, strategies, and resources found on AskOutrageously.com are designed to help you make those big requests and dramatically improve your results. Please check them out and go ask for those outrageous results!

**Assessments**

How Well Do You Ask

What's Their DEAL

What's My DEAL

**Resources and Tools**

Ask Outrageously Survey Results

Asking Tactics and Counter-Requests

Focus Your Ask Form

Identify Strengths and Talents Checklist

Knock Your Asking Block Activity

Master in Request Certificate

Official Permission Slip to Ask

Outrageous Request Form

Share the Load: Meaningful Ways You Can Offer to Help

Spot Your Asking Block Activity

Tips for Starting a Mastermind or Peer Advisory Group

Ways You Can Help a Caregiver

What You Can Ask For at Work Check List

## Media

"If I Were Brave" by Jana Stanfield and Jimmy Scott (Download Song)

"The World Needs You to Ask Outrageously," TEDxSMU talk

## Articles, Media Appearances, and Blog Posts

In addition, a wide variety of strategic resources and secret tools are posted regularly. Please stay connected for current tips and fun news.

To Connect: Follow Linda through Twitter @LindaSwindling and/or use #AskOutrageously.

Also, go to AskOutrageously.com. You can use the links to post to our Facebook and LinkedIn communities. If you participated in the Ask Outrageously challenge, use it to brag about your outcomes. Please Tweet and/or post to let others know about your requests and results. And … tell us who helped you and how you learned to ask for more. You never know how you may encourage others to Ask Outrageously!

# Are You a Smart Ask?

### Want to try the Ask Outrageously Challenge?

Great! You have two days (48 hours) from right now to ask at least three times for something outrageous. At least two need to be professionally related. Make your asks, then report your results.

Or: Take a picture or make a video of you and your copy of this book doing an outrageous activity you've really wanted to try but that's a stretch outside your comfort zone? Skydive? Scuba? Speak in front of an audience? Write a letter to the editor? See a volcano? Talk to a store manager? Go on a date? Babysit your sister's kids? Do it, then post about your outrageous adventure. *Yes*, you have to take a picture or make a video.

**Disclaimer.** It should go without saying, but asking outrageously means asking outside your comfort zone, not risking life or limb. Also, please keep the posted results clean and classy—suitable for a corporate audience. If there's a disclaimer, you know there's a reason for it.

### How do you report your results?

Report your requests and outcomes on AskOutrageously. com or you can use the social media links to post or tweet #AskOutrageously. If you participated in a past challenge, you can reveal your "secret" identity and claim credit for an Outrageous result identified in the book. Please post and get the recognition you're due!

### *Want to be a real smart ask?*

Watch the TEDxSMU video "The World Needs You to Ask Outrageously" at AskOutrageously.com. The stories will help you think of what to ask for and how to ask!

# DEAL Styles and Conversation Strategies

DEAL styles correlate with commonly recognized styles of communication. The chart on page 216 identifies each DEAL style plus popular profiles and assessments that relate to it.

## Development Areas for Each DEAL Style

Below are tips to develop skills for each DEAL style. Review assessments you've taken previously. Even if they don't map precisely, you can use those tools to improve your communication and results when making requests. If you use a communication profile to develop others, you'll find its resources and recommendations will complement the DEAL suggestions below.

### Deciders
*Improve* Deciders' asking skills through training and coaching in communication, patience, sensitivity, and trusting others.
*Enhance* their natural strengths in negotiations, influence, risk taking, and decision making.

### Engagers
*Improve* Engagers' asking skills through training and coaching in impulse control, planning, internal validation, and time management.
*Enhance* their natural strengths in networking, public speaking, and creativity.

### Accommodators
*Improve* Accommodators' asking skills through training and coaching in assertiveness, self-care, independent decision making, and public speaking.
*Enhance* their natural strengths in team building, conflict resolution, and listening.

### Leveragers
Improve Leveragers' asking skills through training and coaching in relaxation, flexibility, letting go of perfectionism, and emotional intelligence.
Enhance natural strengths in planning, strategy, project management, and organization.

# DEAL Styles

| DEAL Style | Neutral Traits | Related Communication Styles |
|---|---|---|
| **Deciders**<br>*When asking, remember:*<br>No chit-chat, don't waste time<br>*Ask about* bottom line, politely challenge thinking. Give a few choices, let them decide. | Extroverted<br>Assertive<br>Serious<br>Intuitive<br>Thinkers<br>Task-oriented | Choleric /Hippocrates<br>Commander/CORE MAP<br>ENT/Myers-Briggs<br>Director/Dominance/DiSC<br>Knower/BrainStyles<br>Red/Personal Insight Inventory<br>Dominance/Predictive Index |
| **Engagers**<br>*When asking remember:*<br>Connect before details/facts<br>*Ask for* input and creative ideas. Will help communicate and engage others— you must follow up. | Extroverted<br>Bold<br>Casual<br>Intuitive<br>Feeling<br>Relationship-oriented | Sanguine/Hippocrates<br>Entertainer/CORE MAP<br>ENF/Myers-Briggs<br>Inducement/Influence/DiSC<br>Conceptor/BrainStyles<br>Yellow/Personal Insight Inventory<br>Extrovert/Predictive Index |
| **Accommodators**<br>*When asking remember:*<br>Relate to people before profit<br>*Ask for* insights into personality and best ways to connect. Be considerate and inclusive. | Introverted<br>Reserved<br>Casual<br>Sensing<br>Feelers<br>Relationship-oriented | Phlegmatic/Hippocrates<br>Relater/CORE MAP<br>ISF/Myers-Briggs<br>Sensors/Supportiveness/DiSC<br>Conciliator/BrainStyles<br>Blue/Personal Insight Inventory<br>Patience/Predictive Index |
| **Leveragers**<br>*When asking remember:*<br>Efficiency over engagement.<br>*Ask about* process, attempts, best practices. Allow time to think. Need details and evidence. | Introverted<br>Reserved<br>Serious<br>Sensing<br>Thinkers<br>Task-oriented | Melancholy/Hippocrates<br>Organizer/CORE MAP<br>IST/Myers-Briggs<br>Compliance/Conscientiousness/DiSC<br>Deliberator/BrainStyles<br>Green/Personal Insight Inventory<br>Formality/Predictive Index |

# Acknowledgments

This book would not have been possible without Zan Jones and her invaluable insight, resources, support, and challenge to show up more outrageously. Thank you, Dianna Booher, for originally giving me the idea I could write a book and for all the introductions, wisdom, encouragement, and years of friendship. Hugs and thanks to Ginger Shelhimer, whose counsel, editing, encouragement, and practical advice are priceless. To Connie Podesta, thanks for suggesting that my topic of negotiation wasn't big enough. And to Howard Putnam and Mark Sanborn, who outrageously asked that the book be *dedicated* to them, I hope you'll accept this *acknowledgment* of your expertise, support, and mentoring.

Thank you to TEDxSMU and Heather Hankamer for giving me the privilege to speak on *The World Needs You to Ask Outrageously*. Who knew a conversation about a picture of Jay Leno would create such outrageous results? My TEDx experience and much more are owed to Dave Lieber, whose encouragement, frankness, and advice are priceless. Lorri Allen, Christine Cashen, Sally Dickson, Hayley Foster, Pamela Jett, and

Elizabeth McCormick, thank you for your suggestions and cheerleading throughout the process. Thank you, Tracy Brown, Candace Fitzpatrick, Ruby Newell-Legner, and Gary Rifkin for your support.

A big shout-out to the BK team: Neal Malliett, Steve Piersanti, and Jeevan Sivasubramaniam. Your leadership, editorial advice, and questions helped make this a much better book. Copy editors Steven Hiatt and Susan Lang for your suggestions and eagle eyes. Reviewers Jane Casperson, Roger Peterson, and Jenny Williams for your editorial suggestions and advice. Thank you Lasell Whipple and your team for the effort and care you gave in creating the cover and graphics. Michael Crowley, Maria Jésus Aguilo, Shabnam Banerjee-McFarland, Kristen Frantz, Catherine Lengronne, and Katie Sheehan, let's outrageously share this book to everyone who needs it! Thank you Anders Renee and Ginger Winters for the BK family welcome.

Thanks to an incredible expert panel of psychologists, psychiatrists, human resources professionals, communication specialists, negotiation experts, leaders, and specialists in organizational behavior. Those who helped identify why people don't ask and what to do about it include John Patrick Dolan, Kip Eads, Kris Harrison, Don Hutson, Robin Lewis, Suzanne Livingston, Gina Morgan, Elaine Morris, Brandon Walker, Nancy Wendeborn and Steve Zimmel, with special appreciation to Dr. Sherry Buffington and Dr. Mel Whitehurst for your time and expert advice on how people communicate, interact, and think. Any errors are entirely mine.

Thank you to the more than 1,163 people who completed the survey and shared your experiences and solutions in making requests. You'll see your contributions throughout. Thank you to all the people who sent me research and forwarded this survey to their circles of friends.

Special thanks to those who went beyond the call of duty including Betty Garrett, Maura Gast, Cindy Hartner, Mellanie Hills, Rexanne Ingram, Kathy Keys, Sally Pasquale, Jill Schiefelbein, Marilyn Sherman, Elénie Tsarhopoulos, Mikki Williams, and Jamie Windle. Your suggestions and doses of encouragement kept me sane.

For exceeding my requests to get the word out, thank you especially to Michelle Adams, Mark Allen, Terri Barrett, Kerry L. Billingsley, Tracy Brown, Evan Carlson, Randy Carlson, June Cline, Michelle Cola, Diana Damron, Steven Davis, Suzanne Davis, Sherry Delagarza, Pegine Echevarria (who *wrote my post* requesting survey participants when I was hesitant to ask), Penny Glasscock, Tamara Hamilton, Deborah Herrington, Olivia Frazer Kerr, Mike Link, Dante Lopez, Mary Marcdante, Melinda Marcus, Hariett Meyerson, Katie Nall, Alyson Beasely Northen, Anna Parkins, Cathy Bench Peterson, Farheen (Seyda) Rizvi, Cathy Rogers, Susan Shapiro, Cheryl Smith, Joe Solinski, Patty Stern, Shannon Teter, Wade Thomas, Susan Tidwell, Sunny Heesun Yun, Brian Vinson (who shared it with five thousand of our high school alumni), Sandy Weaver, Vanessa Vaughter Weilage, and Wendy Winkeler.

Thank you to those who provided success stories and advice on asking outrageously who are mentioned elsewhere or are keeping their superhero identity secret.

Thank you to my friends and colleagues at the National Speakers Association, Power Women of NSA, and NSA North Texas. Through the years you continue to support those of us who believe the notion of writing books and speaking for a living is possible. Thank you to my choir and church friends at Aldersgate UMC who prayed for me and to the Hebron High School Cheer coaches and parents who stepped in when needed. Thanks to the Vistage community, my Trusted Adviser allies, the Breakfast Bunch, and to my Diamonds tribe for showing me that breakthroughs are possible for people and their organizations.

Thank you to my clients and partners in asking, especially to Ericsson, Inc., the outrageously great Irving CVB and Irving Convention team, my Intentional Living Radio workplace family, the amazing gang at J&S Audio Visual, Professional Retail Store Maintenance Association, and those who called attention to the topic and helped develop solutions that work. Thank you to Tim Cocklin, Hugh Culver, Phil Gerbyshak, Phil Reinhardt, Ford Saeks, and Kimberly Wadsworth who help me with my online presence and a bunch of other technical things I wish I understood. Thanks Jimi Willis for making sure "real" work continued.

A special thank you to Jay Leno and the folks at Big Dog Productions! You showed me the importance of asking first for what I really want. Later, you graciously showed me how to achieve outrageous outcomes when I continue to ask. Thank you to my friend Colette Carlson, who arranged for a group of speaker colleagues to attend that fated *Tonight Show* so many years ago.

Many of these lessons and suggestions began with the professors at Texas Tech University, who encouraged leadership and asking outrageously. President of the Ex-Students Association and Communications professor Bill Dean, thank you for your personal mentoring and ability to envision a much bigger future than I thought possible. To Texas Tech's School of Law former assistnat dean, Joseph B. Conboy, thank you for your wisdom and kindess in tough situations. And to the esteemed and widely published professor of commercial law, John E. Kramer, thank you for reinforcing the principle that there are no "stupid" questions.

Finally, a special thank you to my family. Pat and Byron Byars, my mom and dad, are always my encouragers and best editors. My brother Trey Byars, my sister Karen Anne Hall, my sis and bro-in-law Stacy and Tim Mackey, and to Ian, Laura, and Zoe for your support and insight and showing me how to ask outrageously. To Taylor, Parker, and Victoria, thank you for making our family outstanding and all the blessings you've given me *including* your outrageous requests. And to Gregg, you are my confidant, best friend, and biggest supporter. You asked me the best question ever when you asked me to marry you, and my smartest decision ever was saying yes. Here's to many more outrageous years together!

# Index

# About the Author

From the courtroom to the boardroom, Linda Byars Swindling, JD, is an authority in high-stakes communications, negotiating at work, and influencing decision makers. Her specialty is helping people communicate powerfully so that others will listen.

Linda first learned to ask outrageously in the hospitality industry and as a reporter. As an attorney and a mediator, she became an expert in helping others get what they really wanted. When her first book was released in 2000, Linda left her legal practice to focus full-time on Journey On, her Dallas-based, woman-owned business renowned for customized leadership and communication programs, consulting, and executive coaching. Linda delivers keynote speeches and workshops at corporate and association meetings, events, and conventions.

Linda spent five years with Vistage, the world's premier chief executive officer (CEO) development organization. In her role as a chair, she advised and mentored CEOs and decision makers in both one-on-one settings and groups. Linda continues to speak and moderate programs for Vistage. She has received training from the University of Houston's A. A. White Institute for Dispute Resolution and Harvard Law School's Program on Negotiation.

A Certified Speaking Professional and Board Certified Coach, Linda is the author or coauthor of more than twenty books including *Stop Complainers and Energy Drainers: How to Negotiate Work Drama to Get More Done; The Manager's High-Performance Handbook: How to Drive Winning Performance with Everyone on Your Team;* and *The Consultant's Legal Guide.* She is also the creator of the popular *Passports to Success* book series, which offers thirteen titles on workplace and communication issues, including *Get What You Want, Say It Right, Learn to Communicate,* and *Reach Your Goals.* Her clients include Fortune 500 companies as well as many international associations. An award-winning presenter, Linda served as an officer of the National Speakers Association and is a past president of the National Speakers Association of North Texas.

Linda's TEDxSMU talk, "Why the World Needs You to Ask Outrageously," was vetted through an extensive multilevel, peer- and public-reviewed audition process and can be seen on YouTube.

# Berrett–Koehler
## Publishers

**Berrett-Koehler** is an independent publisher dedicated to an ambitious mission: *Connecting people and ideas to create a world that works for all.*

We believe that the solutions to the world's problems will come from all of us, working at all levels: in our organizations, in our society, and in our own lives. Our BK Business books help people make their organizations more humane, democratic, diverse, and effective (we don't think there's any contradiction there). Our BK Currents books offer pathways to creating a more just, equitable, and sustainable society. Our BK Life books help people create positive change in their lives and align their personal practices with their aspirations for a better world.

All of our books are designed to bring people seeking positive change together around the ideas that empower them to see and shape the world in a new way.

And we strive to practice what we preach. At the core of our approach is Stewardship, a deep sense of responsibility to administer the company for the benefit of all of our stakeholder groups including authors, customers, employees, investors, service providers, and the communities and environment around us. Everything we do is built around this and our other key values of quality, partnership, inclusion, and sustainability.

This is why we are both a B-Corporation and a California Benefit Corporation—a certification and a for-profit legal status that require us to adhere to the highest standards for corporate, social, and environmental performance.

We are grateful to our readers, authors, and other friends of the company who consider themselves to be part of the BK Community. We hope that you, too, will join us in our mission.

### A BK Life Book

BK Life books help people clarify and align their values, aspirations, and actions. Whether you want to manage your time more effectively or uncover your true purpose, these books are designed to instigate infectious positive change that starts with you. Make your mark!

To find out more, visit **www.bkconnection.com**.

# Berrett–Koehler
## Publishers

Connecting people and ideas
to create a world that works for all

Dear Reader,

Thank you for picking up this book and joining our worldwide community of Berrett-Koehler readers. We share ideas that bring positive change into people's lives, organizations, and society.

**To welcome you, we'd like to offer you a free e-book.** You can pick from among twelve of our bestselling books by entering the promotional code BKP92E here: http://www.bkconnection.com/welcome.

When you claim your free e-book, we'll also send you a copy of our e-newsletter, the *BK Communiqué*. Although you're free to unsubscribe, there are many benefits to sticking around. In every issue of our newsletter you'll find

- A free e-book
- Tips from famous authors
- Discounts on spotlight titles
- Hilarious insider publishing news
- A chance to win a prize for answering a riddle

Best of all, our readers tell us, "Your newsletter is the only one I actually read." So claim your gift today, and please stay in touch!

Sincerely,

Charlotte Ashlock
Steward of the BK Website

Questions? Comments? Contact me at bkcommunity@bkpub.com.

MIX
From responsible

Certified

**B**

**Corporation**
bcorporation.net